From The Ash

Joe Kidd

ISBN:1533478279
ISBN-13: 978-1533478276

CONTENTS

ACKNOWLEDGMENTS

This book is based on personal experience. My wife and I experienced a home fire first hand early recently. The ordeal was both life-shattering and life-changing. Fortunately, everyone was able to get out of the house safely. While life-shattering, everything, but a few precious photographs, could be replaced. We found that being displaced, not having anything but the clothes on our backs and not knowing where we were going to sleep was more than terrible.

But in our despair, we rediscovered family, community and neighbors. As our house burned many of our neighbors rushed to help and offer assistance, from a caring thought, warm coat and offer of a room for the night to use of tools helping in recovery and rebuilding. The local fire department with the assistance of units from other nearby communities, tirelessly worked to save that which they could including nearly all of our photographs. My son opened his home up to us as a temporary place to stay until we could get our minds around the situation.

We offer are our sincere thanks to all that cared and helped -
     Our neighbors, those were the first on the scene
     Local firefighters, for minimizing our lost
     My son, for offering up his home
     Our insurance company, for their speedy response
     Their claims adjuster, for her diligent efforts
     And those companies that brought our life back together:
          Property recovery and restoration
          Laundry Services
          Restoration contractor and sub-contractors

To you, we offer this work, a chronicle of lessons learned and precautions that can be taken.

From the ash, hope for you..

1 Be Prepared

Chances are either you or someone you know will be impacted by a fire at some stage in their life. Think the unthinkable, and plan for the unplanned. The Boy Scouts have two words for this - Be Prepared.

Fires are more common than you think. In the United States, in 2014:
- A residential fire was reported every 86 seconds
- Someone was injured in a residential fire every 33 minutes.
- Some died in a residential fire every 2 hours and 41 minutes.

Fires are not only things that happen to 'someone else'. They could happen to you, and/or to someone close to you. So please do read and act upon the information here, and encourage your family and friends to do the same.

Create Family Fire Escape Plan

1.   Draw a simple floor plan of your house. This does not have to be to scale and you do not have to include furniture. Do include windows and doors in each room. Also, use one page per floor. Do not try to draw in 3-D. Graph paper can assist you with this.

2.   Mark the first way out of every room in your house. This is usually the door. The first way out should be the way you typically enter the room.

3.   Using a different color crayon or pen mark the second way out of every room. In most rooms it will be a window. It should be the second most direct way out of the room to the outside. Avoid going through other rooms if at all possible. The window would be an option even if the room is on the second floor and very high (see tips and tricks if this applies to you).

4.   With your plan in hand, walk through the house. Check every window that you marked as an exit on your plan. Be sure they open properly and easily. Make sure furniture or other items do not block these exits. Check every door. Make sure they can be opened easily if closed. Check the exit doors you plan to use to the outside (front door, back door, basement door, etc.). Make sure they do not have furniture or other items on the inside blocking them as an exit. Make sure there is not landscaping or other items on the outside that make them hard to use as an exit. Be sure locks and handles work properly and easily.

5.   Choose a rally point in front of the house. This needs to be something permanent like a tree, lamppost, the neighbor's porch, a mailbox, etc. Do not choose things with wheels such as automobiles, RVs and boats. They can easily be moved and may not be there when you need them. This could confuse younger children. Make sure the location is a spot where you can easily be seen by the fire department when they arrive. You can always move to another location once you've let the fire department know that everyone is out safe.

6.   Hold a family meeting to review the plan. Explain to each member of the family what their role

is if there is a fire (who gets the baby, helps grandma, etc.). Make sure each member of the family understands the two exits from their bedroom. Have each family member go to their room and demonstrate that they can open the necessary windows and doors. Make sure each family member understands how locks and handles on outside doors operate. Have them demonstrate that they can open them.

7.   Post the plan in a place where the whole family can see it on a regular basis. The refrigerator, family bulletin board or office is a good location. Smaller children especially may benefit from having a plan of their own posted on the wall in their bedroom.

8.   Have regular fire drills to practice the plan.

9.   Review the plan on a regular basis, at least two times a year. A good suggestion is to review it whenever the seasons change. You will be more likely to discover windows that are swollen shut or doors that are blocked by overgrown landscaping.

Tips and tricks for a successful fire escape plan.

Working smoke detectors are your first line of defense. They will give you early warning that there is a problem. Be sure you have at least one on every level of your house.

Be sure that everyone in the household understands that once you are out of the house, you stay out. No one goes back in for any reason.

Be sure everyone understands to leave everything and get out. Don't waste precious time looking for things. Just leave.

Pets are precious, but they are not worth your life. Many times dogs and cats will find their own way out. Don't waste time looking for a pet. Get out and tell the fire department that your pet is still inside. Be ready to describe where the pet may be (especially if they might be hiding).

If you are on the second floor and there is too much smoke and/or fire for you to exit the normal way, close the door and stick something like a towel or clothing in the crack under the door. Next, go to the window and open it. Take the screen out if you can. If there is a telephone in the room call 9-1-1 and tell them where you are, even if you can hear the fire trucks nearby. The dispatchers will relay the message to the fire responders. Make lots of noise at the window to call attention to the fact that you need help.

If someone in your house is a heavy sleeper, give a lighter sleeper in the household a whistle to blow in an emergency. The extra noise will help rouse them.

Small children sometimes enjoy having their very own copy of the family plan in their room. It is a good reminder for them and gives them a feeling of ownership.

Place a flashlight in each bedroom. Store it on the floor next to the bed. This will give everyone a little added sense of security.

Have a safety check day once a month and get the whole family involved. Adults can test the smoke and carbon monoxide detectors. Teens and tweens can test safety devices on vehicles such as headlights, emergency and turn signal flashers and brake lights. Younger children can test flashlights and change the batteries or bring them to you for a battery change.

Make it a rule that no one disables a smoke detector for any reason. If the detector sounds because of smoke from cooking or steam, waive a towel or magazine under it until it stops sounding.

Avoid fires in the first place by using electrical and heating equipment properly. While cooking, stay with what you are cooking. Don't leave burning candles unattended. Most importantly, keep fire tools such as lighters and matches in a secure place locked away from small children.

Preparation Essentials

Escape Ladder

Consider every room in your house and ask yourself the question "How will I exit this room if the main way out is blocked by fire?" If the answer is 'jump out an upper floor window' you better get an emergency escape ladder for each room on any above ground level floor. While most people can safely jump six feet, you're risking serious injury from a third floor window.

If you buy an escape ladder, practice using it so you know how it works. The wrong time to take it out of its box for the first time is when there's a fire crackling hungrily on the other side of your door.

Also store it near the exit window and make it accessible. It would be of any help if you can find it.

You should also plan on having an extension ladder outside that can be used to reach the windows of the other rooms from the ground outside the house.

Remember, if you have children in another bedroom, it is better for you to leave the house then go around to their window, rather than to struggle through a house on fire.

House Numbering and Visibility

Is your house well numbered, so that it can be read from the street both during the day and at night? Investing in a bright large numbered sign can save valuable seconds or minutes, and if it is an emergency response where you're not able to go to the street to help the Fire or Paramedics to find your location, it might save your life, too.

Consider getting either a solar powered sign or light to make it really stand out at night.

Flashlights

If a fire happens at night you're going to need flashlights. Keep special 'emergency' flashlights in a specific location or locations, somewhere separate from regular house flashlights, and change their batteries every year. Flashlights with LED type bulbs are more reliable than ones with regular incandescent bulbs - the bulbs last much longer.

Fire Extinguisher

You will want to purchase an ABC approved fire extinguisher for your kitchen. It can put out all three levels of fires. Also, it is a smart idea to have at least one fire extinguisher on each level of your home as well as your garage and basement.

Fire Safe

Buy a decent fire safe and put things in there that you cannot replace or do not want to replace. Place these items in plastic zipper bags. If you do not, water from fire hoses will penetrate the safe and get everything inside wet.

Copy computer data and make backups frequently of important photos, data and other things you may have. Keep these in the safe and/or at another location such as your parents' or sibling's home or in a safe deposit box.

Smoke Detectors

Everyone knows that smoke detectors save lives. But are they were they need to be.

When I had my fire, none of the smoke detectors sounded until after I'd already discovered the fire myself. I was alerted to it by the garage door going up.

Lesson learned - put smoke detectors everywhere in your house. Every bedroom should have a smoke detector. The hall connecting the bedrooms should have a smoke detector. Every room you spend significant time in should have a smoke detector. The hall connecting the bedrooms should have a smoke detector. Don't forget the laundry room and near the HVAC and water heater.

You should always sleep with your door closed, and with a fire detector outside the door. That way, if the alarm goes off, you have a more time before the fire appears inside your bedroom. When the alarm sound, don't open your bedroom door before checking the handle and the upper part of the door surface - if there is any warmth, you absolutely don't want to open that door, because the fire is way too close to it on the other side. Exit your bedroom some other way. If you have children in another bedroom, it is better for you to leave the house then go around to their window, rather than to struggle through a house on fire.

Consider placing an ionization type smoke detector for the kitchen. This type of smoke detector uses a miniscule radioactive source and tests for ionization for gaseous by-products of a fire faster, and smoke slower. These will have fewer false alarms for burning toast.

Most smoke detectors have low battery warning alerts, but remember to change the batteries at least twice a year. Also once a year actually test your smoke detector to make certain that it works. The best test is to actually burn a small piece of paper in a safe heat resistant container and hold the container just below the smoke detector. If it takes a while for the alarm to sound, make plans to replace it.

Smoke alarm manufacturers recommended you change your smoke detectors every ten years. You can write the purchase date in the battery compartment and check it each time you replace the battery.

Even new detectors can quickly fail. A recent study showed that 20% of ionization type alarms had failed within 9 months. Don't take a chance with your safety test your smoke alarm frequently.

2 Be Protected

When shopping for home insurance, there's much more to consider than how much your coverage will cost.

You need to buy the right type of policy.

You need the proper level of protection, plus special provisions for valuables such as jewelry, your computer equipment and other possessions.

You might also need additional coverage for such things as earthquakes or flooding.

Lending institutions usually require mortgage customers to purchase homeowner's insurance. Don't rely on the coverage levels mandated by your bank or mortgage company. Those levels are designed to protect the house itself, but not necessarily your possessions. That's why it's important to check with your agent or insurance company to make sure you have adequate coverage.

The terms of standard home insurance policies have been industry defined, so standard coverage is not going to vary from company to company, although rates will. There are three primary types of situations that enable a homeowner or renter to be eligible for a policy:

- Owner-occupants of private homes: Individuals and families who own the private home in which they reside.
- Tenants of residential premises: People who rent or lease the premises where they reside.
- Owners and owner-occupants of residential condominium units: Individuals and families who own private condominium units used for residential purposes.

Homeowner's policies can also provide limited property coverage for incidental occupancy, which is the use of the residential premises for purposes not residential (such as a home office or studio). This can be done only as long as two requirements are met: the premise must be occupied principally as a dwelling, and the premise cannot be used for any business purpose other than the incidental occupancy.

Basic policies

Each homeowner's policy provides a combination of property and liability coverage and covers loss of use resulting from damage. There are several basic types of home insurance policies:

A broad homeowner's policy- covers house and contents against 16 perils.

- Fire or lightning
- Windstorm or hail
- Explosion
- Riot or civil commotion
- Damage caused by aircraft
- Damage caused by vehicles
- Smoke
- Vandalism or malicious mischief

- Theft
- Volcanic eruption
- Falling objects
- Weight of ice, snow, or sleet
- Accidental discharge or overflow of water or steam from within a plumbing, heating, air conditioning, or automatic fire-protective sprinkler system, or from a household appliance.
- Sudden and accidental tearing apart, cracking, burning, or bulging of a steam or hot water heating system, an air conditioning or automatic fire-protective system.
- Freezing of a plumbing, heating, air conditioning or automatic, fire-protective sprinkler system, or of a household appliance.
- Sudden and accidental damage from artificially generated electrical current (does not include loss to a tube, transistor or similar electronic component).

Special homeowner's policy - covers all perils except those specifically excluded by the policy.

Renter's policy - covers the 16 above named perils and includes liability coverage. It does not insure the dwelling itself.

For owners of co-ops or condominiums - provides personal property coverage, liability coverage and specific coverage of improvements to the owner's unit. Insurance provided by the owner's association normally covers most of the actual structure.

Your Policy

Every homeowner's policy has three preliminary sections (declarations page, general agreement, and definitions) as well as two coverage sections (Coverage A, B, C, or D).

In the preliminary section, the declarations page contains the policy number, period of coverage, insured's name and address, agent's name, limits that apply to the coverage, additional insureds (if any), premium amount, etc.

The general agreement works as a preface to the entire policy and states that the insurer's coverage and obligations to the consumer depend solely on the insured's ability to pay the premiums and comply with the policy's guidelines.

The definitions section contains multiple parts.

The first part explains that "you" and "your" in the policy refer to the named insured, while instances of "we," "us," and "our" refer to the insurance company. The second part lists and defines commonly used terms associated with the policy and the coverage.

Buying Homeowners Insurance

When you apply for homeowner's insurance, you will be asked provide a great deal of information. The insurance company will ask you about your current occupation and employment history, marital status, previous addresses, date of birth and Social Security number. The insurer will check your criminal, credit, and insurance history to see if you are a "good risk." The insurance company also will look at your "loss history" to see what kinds of home insurance claims you've made in the past.

Then you'll have to decide what type of homeowner's policy you want, your preferred deductible, and how you'll pay for the coverage (in full or in installments). Your agent or insurance company will determine how much it would cost to replace your house and many of the items inside. For more expensive property, such as jewelry and computer equipment, you will need special coverage in addition to the basic policy.

Analyzing your home

Many factors go into determining the premiums for a homeowner's policy. The age of your home, the materials used to build it, where it's located, the square footage, and the numbers of rooms, all play a role.

How do you heat your home? What's the overall condition of the house? How many people live in your home? How close is your home to the nearest fire station and fire hydrant? The answers to these questions also help determine how much you'll pay for your homeowner's policy.

The insurer will be able to give you an estimate for rebuilding your house in the event of a total loss. Remember, this is the rebuilding cost based on local construction costs, not the market value of your home.

Ways to save

If your home is equipped with an alarm system, smoke detectors and deadbolt locks, you could save money. Those items help make your home safer and more secure. If you have an in-ground pool or a trampoline, you might pay higher premiums. Removing trees from striking distance of the residence can also help save cash. You can also expect to pay more if you are located in a higher risk area, such as a coastline. Your insurance company will also want to know if you plan to use the home for any business purposes, of if you plan to rent all or part of the house, both of which can increase liability.

Armed with all this information, insurance companies determine how much to charge you for insurance.

Your policy's dollar limits are important.

If you insure your house for $100,000, that's the most you will get if it is destroyed, even if it would cost more to replace it. The Declarations Page on the front of your policy shows how much coverage you have. Talk with your agent or company representative if you have any questions about your insurance limits. Don't wait until you have a claim to learn your policy's limit.

Replacement cost coverage for your personal property

The extent of coverage provided on various homeowner's policies depends on the loss settlement clause. This clause identifies property that will be valued at actual cash value, and property that will be valued at replacement cost.

Before buying homeowners insurance, you need to understand the difference between "replacement cost" and "actual cash value."

Homeowner's policies automatically cover household contents — furniture, clothes, appliances, etc. — up to 40 percent of the amount your house is insured for. This means if you insure your house for $100,000, its contents are insured for up to $40,000. You can get more coverage by paying a higher premium. This automatic coverage pays only the actual cash value of damaged, stolen, or destroyed household goods. Actual cash value is an item's replacement cost, minus depreciation.

Replacement cost policies give you more protection than actual cash value coverage. For example, what happens if a burglar steals your six-year-old television set? With actual cash value coverage, you get only what you would expect to pay for a six-year-old television set. With replacement cost coverage, the insurance company pays to replace your TV with a new set similar to the stolen one.

Guaranteed replacement cost coverage pays for the full cost of replacing or repairing a damaged or destroyed home, even if it is above the policy limit.

Extended replacement cost coverage pays a certain amount above the policy limit to replace a damaged home, generally 120 or 125 percent. It is similar to a guaranteed replacement cost policy, which has no percentage limits. Most homeowner policy limits track inflation in building costs. Guaranteed and extended replacement cost policies are designed to protect the policyholder after a major disaster when the high demand for building contractors and materials can push up the normal cost of reconstruction.

Ask about discounts for:
- Multi-policy (home, car or other policies with the same company)
- Smoke detectors
- Fire extinguishers
- Sprinkler systems
- Burglar and fire alarms that alert an outside service
- Deadbolt locks and fire-safe window grates
- 55 years old and retired
- Long-time policyholder
- Upgrades to plumbing, heating and electrical systems
- Earthquake retrofitting to make the home safer
- Wind-resistant shutters

Take inventory

Many people learn after a fire or storm they didn't have enough personal property coverage. Taking inventory will help you decide how much insurance you need. It also will simplify claims.

Your inventory should list each item, its value, and serial number. Photograph or videotape each room, including closets, open drawers, storage buildings, and your garage. Keep receipts for major items in a fireproof place.

What other protections does my policy provide?

Homeowner's policies regularly provide other types of coverage, including off-premises theft protection and unauthorized use of your credit cards. Make sure you understand which provisions are included in the standard coverage you elect to purchase and which might require supplemental premiums.

Supplemental coverage

Homeowner's policies cover specific risks. Depending on what you own and where you live, you might need to supplement your policy with special coverage.

Flood insurance

Homeowner's policies do not cover flood damage. The National Flood Insurance Program (NFIP) offers flood coverage in many areas. Local insurance agents sell NFIP flood policies and can tell you about the program in your area, or you can contact the NFIP at (888) 379-9531.

If a mortgage lender determines a home is in a special flood hazard area, the borrower might be required to purchase flood insurance.

Extra coverage (endorsements)

Homeowner's policies contain exclusions and limitations for some types of personal property that are particularly susceptible to loss. Some homeowner's policies place a specific dollar limit on certain property such as jewelry or antiques.

You might want more coverage for certain items than your policy provides. For an extra premium, you can buy endorsements that expand or increase the coverage on these items. Some of the most common endorsements cover jewelry, fine arts, camera equipment, coin or stamp collections, computer equipment, and radio and television satellite dishes and antennas. To insure that these types of items are properly covered, look into a "scheduled personal property endorsement."

A scheduled personal property endorsement is characterized by broad coverage and flexibility. This policy can be purchased separately as a "personal articles floater" policy or endorsed to your homeowner's policy. A floater policy designates coverage for items that are likely to experience frequent movement from one place to another such as (but not limited to) cameras, jewelry, musical instruments, golf equipment, silverware, furs, etc.

Personal umbrella liability insurance

If you want more liability coverage than a homeowner's policy provides, you can buy a separate umbrella policy. Because policies vary, make sure the agent or company fully explains the coverage.

Higher deductibles, lower premiums

Your home insurance deductible is the amount you pay for covered damage before insurance kicks in. You can generally choose a higher deductible in order to lower your premiums if you don't mind taking on the added risk. Ask your insurance agent to give you price quotes for a range of deductibles to see how much you'd save.

Usually a deductible is a flat rate, such as $1,000. But many insurers are introducing "percentage deductibles" around the country, especially for policies covering earthquakes, hurricanes and windstorms. These policies make you liable for 1 to 5 percent of your home's insured value before the insurance company pays. So, if you have a 2 percent deductible and your home's insured value is $250,000 (remember, that's the cost to rebuild, not your home's market value), you'd have to pay the first $5,000 in damages.

Some homeowners are switched from flat-rate to percentage deductibles at renewal time and may not be aware of the change. Make sure to read special notices sent by your home insurer and your "declarations page" at renewal time, or call your agent to check on what kind of deductible you have..

3 Safe and Secure

With your family's safety plan and homeowner's insurance in place, your challenge is to make certain your personal belongings are safe and secure. Experiencing a fire loss is devastating, but imagine trying to list from memory every single item in your home that might be lost. That task is less daunting if you create a home inventory in advance and store it in a safe location. This is a three step process:

- Decide how and where you want to store the inventory.
- Take an inventory of the contents of your home.
- Third and possibly most important, keep the inventory up to date.

How and where you want to store the inventory.

Regardless of how you do it (written list, photos, videos,), keep your inventory along with receipts in a safe and secure location. The likely choices are:

- bank safe deposit box – the inconvenience of access may discourage frequent updates ,
- a relative's home – again access may discourage your updates
- personal computer – your computer could be damaged or destroyed
- smartphone – your phone could be loss or you might forget to transfer data to the new phone.

Better choices are:

- An inventory app for your smartphone or tablet
- a database or spreadsheets of inventory lists
- a simple word document with embedded photos or videos.

Each of these make it easy to keep up to date and have data stored remotely in online backup services, cloud storage accounts or even your personal email account. No matter how your where you store the inventory, make certain it is safe by using password protection or encryption.

Inventory applications

Inventory applications are available on multiple platforms for your computer, smartphone and tablet. We took a look at several free apps that promise to reduce the drudgery associated with this crucial task. We found that some are better than others, but each one provides a means of inventorying your valuable possessions with descriptions, prices, warranty status, and photographs. They also enable you to identify where the objects are located.

Check with your insurance company first as they may have apps available for your use.

- Allstate Digital Locker
- American Family Insurance's DreamVault
- State Farm HomeIndex
- Liberty Mutual Home Gallery

Each of these have similar features and let you take a photo inventory using your iPhone, iPad, or Android device. Some even have the ability to export your inventory as a spreadsheet or PDF for safe storage. They are offered free of charge. See your insurance company's website for more details.

Additionally there are several good quality independent applications that are available multiple platforms. Details for four of the best follow.

- Know Your Stuff

  Know Your Stuff is a free online inventory service provided by the Insurance Information Institute. The site will walk you through configuring rooms in your home and listing the items each, complete with photos and receipts for documentation. The step by step process walks you through everything you need to enter, you can be sure you're recording all of the right information. And, everything is stored online, so you have easy access to your home inventory from anywhere you have an Internet connection.

  Know Your Stuff has the most comprehensive toolset that's available on the web or your mobile device, which makes it our pick for the best digital home inventory service. The app is available for Android, iOS or browser based. Being able to open your inventory in a browser makes adding the details a lot easier, because you can use a real keyboard.

- Encircle

  Encircle, also available for Android, iOS, and via the Web. You start by adding a property (you can have more than one) and then choosing the relevant rooms from a list. To add items in a room, you can photograph them individually, or you can take a photo of the whole room and afterwards tap on each item in the picture. Encircle creates a new item in the list for each tap, and you can add the details later, including a photo of the receipt.

- Inventory for Homeowners

  This picture-driven asset manager allows you to upload photos of your property, useful for visual proof for insurance purposes, but also for landlords or home decor shopping. You can layer on as many details purchase date, price, model and serial numbers. There is no limit to how many pictures or how much information can be added. For Android or iOS.

- The Home Inventory

  This app allows you to keep a home inventory using barcodes with its built-in scanner in addition to uploading photos and information. For Android or iOS.

Not an app person?

If you don't feel like learning an entirely new piece of software to get your home inventory done, that's fine. You can make a home inventory with plenty of different applications—all you really need is a document listing items, values, and serial numbers as well as a place to store photos of your stuff.

Here are a couple of common applications that could pull double duty to manage your home inventory—but if you aren't already using these apps for something else, using Know Your Stuff will probably be the easiest way to go.

- Evernote and OneNote

  Evernote and OneNote let you organize photos and text documents across the web and your mobile devices, which makes it a great way to store inventory photos alongside notes containing additional information. Evernote is available for iOS, Android, Windows Phone and Blackberry devices and as a downloadable desktop app. OneNote is available for Windows Phone, Windows RT, Android, iOS and mobile browsers can access OneNote web app. A desktop version available as well.

- Google Docs
  Google Docs is an online word processing tool that lets you create a basic list of your belongings—and, while it's not the best place to store images, you can add images to your documents for a complete inventory.
- Microsoft Office
  If you are an Office fan, you can use Access to create an inventory database (several templates are available for download), Excel to create a comprehensive spreadsheet inventory (yes, even photos can be added to each worksheet) or Word to create tables holding your inventory and imbed photos in the documents.

We've given you a few great options for creating your home inventory. So, if you don't have a home inventory, put it on your short list. And, whichever service you choose, be sure to be comprehensive and keep it up to date—you'll be glad you did if you're ever faced with filing a claim.

Use a Home Inventory Service

If you don't feel confident about doing the inventory yourself there are home inventory service providers nationwide. This one of the services that I perform through my consulting service. You can use the yellow pages or do internet search to locate a service provider near you. A home inventory may specialize in documenting and recording personal property for homeowners. and can provide you with a complete written, video, and digital photographic record of your home and its contents. When choosing a professional, reliable, third party, home inventory specialist due diligence is must, checking. Make certain your choice is insured, bonded and licensed if required in your state. Also check the local Better Business Bureau for the providers professional history.

Collecting your inventory

There are several ways to approach personal property inventory. The easiest of the approach taken will likely be the most incomplete. A complete inventory may take some time to create and could be updated over time. You will be surprised of the treasures you will find in your own home that you had not thought about. My personal choice starts with taking photographs of each room and then preparing a detailed property list.

Room by room photos.

The old saying "A picture is worth a thousand words" aptly describes my recommended method of starting an inventory. The process is as simple as a walk through your house. Start at your entry door and work your way through the house starting with main living spaces, followed by the kitchen, bedrooms, hallways and baths. Do not forget the garage and basement.

My approach is to stand in the room facing north, take a picture, then face east take a picture, followed by south and west. Then I face northeast, snap photo of the corner of the room and repeat until each corner is photographed. This will allow you of have a simple panoramic look at the whole. The same can be accomplished with a panoramic or video camera. The disadvantage of a video review is the speed and steadiness of the camera.

The following set of illustrations will demonstrate the process:

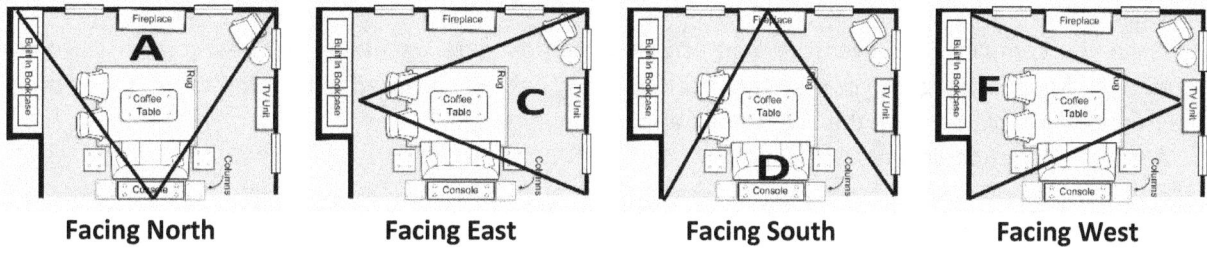

Facing North **Facing East** **Facing South** **Facing West**

Try to capture as much of each wall as space allows. The corner photos will as capture part of the floor and ceiling because of the added depth of the room.

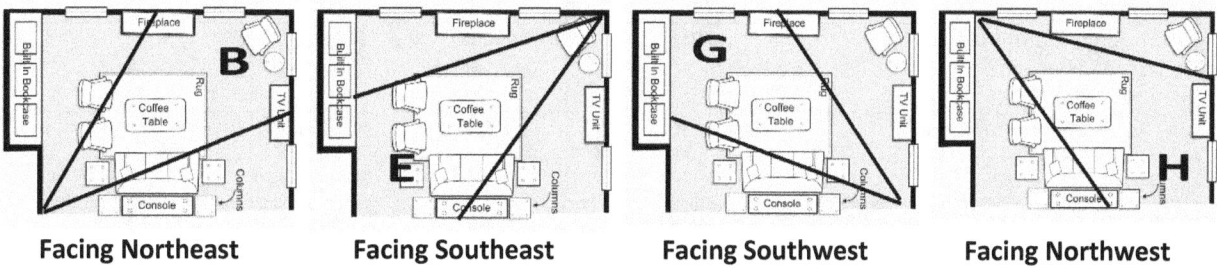

Facing Northeast **Facing Southeast** **Facing Southwest** **Facing Northwest**

Once complete with room, repeat the process until all of the rooms have been photographed. Some rooms like baths and closet may not be large enough to need all eight photos. For instance my master room, I snap a photo at the door and another at the wall across from the door. This will have captured all of the contents of the room.

You may want to take a new set of photos for any room that you move around, redecorate and purchase new items for.

While on the subject of photos, this would be a good time to go outside and take pictures of the exterior using the same approach shown above. This capture all of the hidden features of the house. Additionally, I went to Google Maps and captured the satellite view of house and stored it the other photos.

Your inventory

To begin gathering your inventory, start in the room you took the first photographs. Using whatever system you decided upon, go item by item capturing the following details every visible item:

- description of the item,
- model number, if applicable
- serial number, if applicable
- year purchased
- amount paid and receipt if available.
- quantity, if more than one (i.e. end tables, lamps)
- comments

Don't forget the ceilings, floors and window coverings. This will be a time consuming, but all to important task. Don't become discouraged. To keep the task from being overwhelming, I processed one room each night until complete. At this point, don't inventory the contains of cabinets, closets and drawers.

Once you complete the inventory, you can keep it up to date by adding any new purchases to the room's list. Keep, photograph or scan the receipts of any newly purchased items. Don't forget to remove the item being replaced from the inventory if applicable.

A sample of a room inventory follows:

Media Room – last updated April 2016

Description	Year Purchased	Amount Paid	Have Receipt	Qty	Notes
End Table / Lamp Unit	2008	225.00	Y	2	
Roman Shades / Burgundy	2008	125.00	Y	8	
DVD Rack	2008	10.00	N	1	
65 inch Sony 4K UltraHD LED TV Model #: 123456 Serial #: SYHR65A29	2016	1400.00	Y	1	
Sony 4K UltraHD Blu-ray Player Model #: UHD-8976 Serial #:AWE98701H	2016	345.00	Y	1	
Sony-2.1-Channel Soundbar with Wireless Subwoofer - Black Model: HTST9SKU Serial: 3953262	2016	499.00	Y	1	
Cocktail table42 inch tall with 2 chairs	2008	299.00	Y	1	
Ashley reclining home theater set 2 seat.	2016	800.00	Y	1	
Ashley reclining sofa 2 set	2016	800.00	Y	1	
Ashley leather recliner – electric	2016	800.00	Y	1	
Wall décor pieces	2008	25.00	N	8	
Side table	2016	99.00	Y	1	
ANKER USB Charging station	2016	79.00	Y		
Hampton Island Breeze Ceiling fan	2008	179.00	Y		
Dyson AM07 Tower Fan	2016	499.00	Y		

Cabinets, closets cupboards and drawers

If the first part of the inventory felt daunting, the next part can be really time consuming. Cabinets, closet, cupboards and drawers can contain hundreds of items. To make this simpler, appendix A contains a variety of templates the can be used recording your inventory.

Let's start in the Kitchen, an inventory template follows:

Kitchen

Item	Qty	Description	Cost	Item	Qty	Description	Cost
Answer Machine				Hot Pads			
Answer Tape/Batteries				Ice Cream Maker			
Appetizer Skewers				Ice Cube Trays			
Bakeware				Juice Pitcher			
Baking Trays				Knife Block			
Blender/Electric Mixer				Linen Napkins/Holders			
Bottle Top Opener				Marble Cheese Pad			
Bread Maker				Marjoram/Rosemary			
Broom/Pan/Mop				Measuring Cups			
Bundt Cake Mold				Measuring Spoons			
Butter Dish				Mixing Bowls			
Butter Knives				Muffin Pans			
Can Opener				Olive Knives			
Canisters				Oven Mitts			
Carving Knife/Fork				Paper Bags			
Cheese Grater				Paper Napkins/Towels			
Cheese Knife				Paper Party Plates			
Cheese Plates				Pasta Machine			
Cleaning Bucket				Pasta Strainer			
Cleaning Supplies				Pepper Grinder			
Cleaning Towels				Plastic Storage Tubs			
Cloth Dishtowels				Plasticware			
Coffee Grinder				Pots, Pans, Lids			
Coffeemaker/Filters				Pressure Cooker			
Cookbooks/Holder				Recycling Can			
Cookie Jar				Refrigerator Magnets			
Cookware				Rice Cooker			
Corn Nibs				Rolling Pin			
Cream Server				Rotisserie			
Crock Pot				Salad Spinner			
Cutlery				Salt/Pepper Shakers			
Cutting Boards				Sandwich/Plastic Bags			
Dish Soap/Tray				Sea Salt Mill			
Dish Towels				Serving Spoons			
Dishware				Serving Trays			
Drink Coasters				Shelving/Brackets			
Electric Deep Fryer				Silverware Holder			
Electric Frying Pan				Sink Stopper/Screen			
Electric Griddle				Small Kitchen Utensils			
Electric Grill				Smoke Detector			
Electric Hand Mixer				Soaps/Sponges			

Item	Qty	Description	Cost	Item	Qty	Description	Cost
Electric Juicer				Spatulas/Spoons			
Electric Knife Sharpener				Spice Rack			
Electric Mixer				Sponges/Scrubs/Tray			
Electric Wok				Standing Towel Holder			
Fire Extinguisher				Tablecloths/Runners			
Flatware				Telephone			
Flower Vases				Television			
Fondue Pot				Thermometer			
Food Dehydrator				Thermos/Lunchboxes			
Food Processor				Toaster			
Food Sealer				Toaster Oven			
Foreman Grill				Tortilla Warmer			
Garlic Press				Trash Can/Bags			
Gelatin Molds				Trash Compactor			
Glassware				Trivets			
Gravy Boat				Turkey Baster			
Guacamole Dish				Waffle Iron			
Hand Can Opener				Window Treatments			
Hand Grater				Wine Opener			
Hand Juicer				Wire Cooling Racks			
Hand Soap				Wire Splatter Screen			
Hand Whisks				Other:			

It is important to note that this inventory sheets does not contain consumables. Adding consumables require constant updating and more or your valuable time. Open each cabinet and drawer begin counting every item, record a brief description of the item and what the item cost. This list becomes your starting point, when complete move on to the next category or room. Similar templates are available for all of your personal property, some of which are:

- Apparel for each person in the household
- Accessories
- Jewelry
- Personal items
- Outerwear
- Shoes and boots

Once each of the templates are complete, safely secure the lists. A variety of storage avenues are available; electronic with cloud storage, paper stored in a safe deposit or even on your smart phone or tablet. My preference is electronic with both physical and cloud storage. Having a home business, my livelihood is contained on computers. I store all of my documents, these and everything else on a portable hard drive. The price for these storage devices as come down dramatically over the past few years. I perform daily backups to the hard drive and store it in a fire-rating safe. Additionally, I store my inventory documents inside of a draft email in my Gmail account. This allows for easy access to update or in the event it is needed. The email folder is even more secure than other cloud based options as long as you frequently change passwords and enable two-step authentication.

You are now probably thinking about how to keep the inventory worksheets up to date. I have a system where I keep all of my receipts for anything purchased for the house and on a monthly basis record all of the purchased items. Additionally, I scan the receipts for all big ticket items or take advantage of retailers that send receipts by email (Home Depot, Best Buy, Amazon, etc.) Samples of each worksheets in Appendix A.

Flight or Fight

One additional consideration, given the recent wildfires in the western U.S. and Canada, the massive destruction from tornados in the Midwest and flooding from hurricanes. You need to be prepared in the event of total destruction. The inventory process suggested before is inadequate in this regard.

Begin by getting access to the home appraisal from when you brought the house or last refinanced. Usually there is a sketch or diagram of the general layout of your house. Enlarge that to one room per sheet of paper. If the appraisal is not handy, you can sketch a diagram of each room. Go room by room, adding the overall dimensions and the location of all of the features of the room. This would include light switches, lighting, wall outlets and built in features. Taking pictures or making a video of the same is also a good approach.

One particular area to document is any built in or attached cabinetry. Bath and kitchen cabinetry come in a variety of depths, heights and lengths. Without proper documentation you may end with smaller cabinets. Make no mistake missing 2 inches of depth in a kitchen cabinet is big mistake. I learned from mine. Take pictures of your cabinets with a tape measure in the picture to prove the dimension. Quality of the cabinets and countertops can be proved by photos. I you don't plan for the worst, you will not get the best.

4 The Fire

"The roof, the roof, the roof is on fire" is a song from the 1980's by Rock Master Scott & the Dynamic. Our son listened to the version offered by the Bloodhound Gang over and over and over again. At the time little did we know that this song would hold a place in our future.

Most of us will probably lead our entire lives unaffected by fire. But the savage brutality and lethal destructiveness of fire is so extreme that you need to read the following statement.

"In the case of fire – dial 911 or our local fire department."

It was mid-March and as many college basketball fans we were watching a conference championship game. To make this a special event, I had been smoking ribs on our patio, in spite of being cold with snow flurries. I took the chip pack out of the grill and placed in it on the concrete patio beneath the grill, in order to put a glaze on the ribs at high temperature. After just the right amount of caramelization, I turned the grill off and brought the ribs into the house.

Midway through the third quarter and while eating the ribs, we heard the garage door open. I investigated by opening the door to the garage, not smelling smoke, looked out the back door and saw the exterior wall on fire. Even before the smoke detectors went off, the fire had had made its way through the wall and roof structure.

I yelled to my wife to get everyone out of the house and proceeded to pull the car out of the garage while on the phone with the 911 dispatcher. After parking the car in the middle of the yard, I joined my wife and son at the end of the driveway, our designated rally point.

Within minutes, our neighbors responded to make certain everyone got safe and okay. As we watched the smoke roll out of every side the roof we were joined by neighbors wanting to make certain everyone was safe and okay. In less than 2 minutes, from when the garage door opened, the back half of the house was completely engulfed in flames.

Flight or Fight

Fires are complex, unpredictable, very fast growing, and terribly dangerous. A single spark can become a room fully ablaze in three minutes, and can progress to the entire house ablaze in six minutes.

Even trained firefighters, with proper equipment, will fight a major house fire first from the outside, not the inside.

Fire prevention and firefighters always stress that ordinary untrained people, without special equipment, should never risk themselves fighting a household fire.

The only time you should fight a fire is if you catch a fire in the very first stages of development, you have a fire extinguisher that can be used to contain it and you have a clear path for evacuation it you should not be successful.

Never allow fire, smoke, or heat to get between you and your exit.

Using a Fire Extinguisher

Squirt the extinguisher broadly at the base of the fire. When the fire has stopped, don't stop the extinguisher. Keep squirting short bursts at where the flames where until the extinguisher is empty - a half discharged extinguisher can't be kept for 'next time' and the longer you keep the flames out, the more the area has a chance to cool, and the less likely it is they'll restart when you've stopped spraying them with the powder.

Get everyone out of the house and call of Fire Department

Always call the Fire Department. They are a free resource for us all, paid for by our tax dollars. They truly are the trained professionals, and if you have any type of fire, it is only sensible to call them.

Remember, if you don't call the fire department your homeowners insurance company might dispute your claim, contending that you didn't act prudently, and suggesting that the fire damage might have been less if you'd called them rather than fighting the fire yourself.

Once you are out of the house, gather at your rally point and account for everyone. If someone is missing, tell the fire department. They are better equipped than you to perform the rescue.

Meet the Fire Department on the street

If your house is obscured from the street, or even if it is visible from the street, go and meet the Fire Department on the street. Tell the 911 dispatcher that you will go and flag them down on the street - if at night take a flashlight with you. Spell this out so the message gets radioed on to the fire trucks - say 'tell the fire truck drivers to watch out for me - I'll be waving and jumping up and down on the side of the street'.

This helps the Fire Department because they don't have to slow down and start checking house numbers - they just look for the person waving and jumping up and down!

Summary

A house fire can very quickly transition from insignificant to out of control. If you discover any type of fire, the first thing you should do is ensure the safety of yourself and everyone else in the house.

If you can safely fight the fire yourself, it may be sensible and proper to do so. But no-one will criticize you if you simply evacuate the building.

Some simple preparations and precautions, as mentioned in the first part of this article, can greatly reduce the negative impacts of a fire.

5 What's Next

Take care of yourself and your family

Your first priority should be to take care of yourself and your family. Living through the shock of a disastrous event is a daunting task and it will take some time to get your life back in order. The key ingredient in this phase is to realize that you have a dedicated team of professionals behind you working on your home while you are working on getting your family settled.

Some kind words from friends and neighbors go a long way to start cheering you up. But, you must think of yourself as well as your family. It is important that you manage your schedule and not take on too many things at once. Eat as you would normally do and maintain healthy rest periods as you pick up the pieces. Remember things will get done in a short period of time and your life will soon be back to normal

To get yourself and your family back on track, talk about what's happened. Talking is sometimes the best for the family to work through their problems. As the days go by, knowing it is normal to have various feelings about the disaster, will help you and your family recover from the loss. The burden does not have to lie on your shoulder, there are many resources in your community that will provide you with the support you need as your work through the emotional part of your loss.

Take care of your things.

Secure the property. It's your responsibility as the homeowner to make sure the house is secured against further damage.
- Board up broken windows and smashed doors.
- Cover holes in roof and walls.

In some cases, the Fire Department will secure the property for you, or the municipal housing department will do it. Your insurance policy may pay reasonable expenses incurred in preserving insured property.

If your property is looted, contact the police immediately. Tell them what was stolen. This report may be needed to file an insurance claim for theft, distinct from any disaster damage claim.

Pets can get very frightened in an emergency, if you have lost one; contact your local SPCA or Humane society and your neighbors so they can keep an eye out for your pet.

Notify your mortgage company about the results of the disaster and to keep them informed about what's being done to restore the property. They may have forms for you to fill out, and they may want to inspect the property.

Call your Insurance Company

The first thing you should do after you know you have suffered a loss due to a fire is call your insurance company to notify them that your house burned. You will then need to file a claim. This typically includes: the date of loss, type of loss, location damage, any related injuries, others involved, condition of the home, description of damaged contents, whether or not temporary repairs are necessary and a police report.

Get a replacement copy of your policy and declarations page as soon as possible. Check the stated dollar limits for your main coverage categories:

- Dwelling,
- Other Structures
- Personal property
- Scheduled personal property items, (artwork, electronics, jewelry, valuables)
- Loss of use
- Additional Living Expenses
- Personal Liability
- Medical Payments

Make sure the policy limits accurately reflect the coverage you thought you had purchased. Get a copy of the regulations or laws that govern fair claim settlements in your state from your Department of Insurance and READ THEM!

Get a place to stay.

You have to find a place to stay that is not temporary, at least a week. That may seem short but it establishes a sense of normalcy. With loss of use coverage, your insurance company should provide temporary housing, a hotel room, furnished apartment or a furnished rental comparable to your home. You will still be responsible for paying your mortgage payment. Don't be in rush to settle on temporary housing. Use a hotel for a week of so until you find out how long the repair on your home will take. An apartment might work for a month of two, but you might prefer a house if the repair is going to take longer than three months.

Keep in mind that the choice in temporary housing is yours. Don't be forced temporary housing that is not acceptable of comfortable.

The "loss of use" clause, which entitles you to reimbursement for living expenses while you're out of your home. However, you're entitled only to additional living expenses—that is, the difference between what it costs you to live on a daily basis at home and what it costs now. For example, if you ate most meals at home before the fire and regularly spent $300 a week on groceries, but are now spending $400 per week at restaurants, you can claim only $100.

Maintain copies for your records. If insurance company delays or circumstances beyond your control made the rebuilding or repairs take longer, argue for longer Additional living expenses benefits.

Make notification of your temporary location

- your insurance agent/company
- your mortgage company (also inform them of the fire and keep up on those payments)
- your family and friends
- your employer
- your child's school
- your post office
- any delivery services
- your fire and police departments
- our utility companies

Be organized

When you deal with an insurance company over a major claim, you need to be organized. Get a three ring binder and pocket dividers to help with the task. Documentation is your best friend at the stage.

Create sections in the binder for:

- *Communication*
    - Take notes on every call with your insurance company, adjuster and contractor.
    - Retain copies of every email and letter you send or receive.
- *Receipts*
    - Keep every receipt and cancelled check, it is easier to keep them now rather find them later.
- *Inventory*
    - Your property lists
    - Pre fire photos
    - Damaged property list
    - Post fire photos
    - List of property taken for cleaning, restoration or storage
- *Appraisal*
    - Original appraisal
    - Revised appraisal after inspection (if any)
    - Revised appraisal after clean out
- *Estimates*
    - Contractor estimates
    - Contactor statement of work
    - Final estimate after reconciliation
- *Invoices*
    - *Board up / secure property*
    - *Restoration company*
    - *Storage company*

Keep Paying Those Premiums

It may seem ridiculous to continue paying homeowner's insurance premiums to protect property that's severely damaged or gone, but stopping your payments can be a big mistake. A secondary loss may occur while your home is being repaired or rebuilt.

Remember, your homeowner's policy includes liability protection for you and your household, including your pets. This may come in handy if, for example, your stressed-out dog chews up an expensive Oriental rug while you're camped out at your brother-in-law's house.

If you'll be staying somewhere for a while, call your agent and ask for that address to be added as a second location for purposes of liability coverage. If your home has been destroyed, ask your insurance company to cut back on the part of the policy that covers the structure, and ask for a corresponding reduction in premiums.

Reentering your home

Once you have received the go ahead to reenter your home, proceed with caution, your safety is more important than your things. Chances are the fire department will have your utilities turned off and notify your local building safety department for an inspection to determine if your home is habitable.

Some useful things to bring with you include a flashlight, camera, garbage bags, gloves and safety boots. Only remove your valuables, essential legal documents, identification, medicines and items of sentimental value. Don't begin clean-up until the adjuster from your insurance company sees the damage.

Replacing your immediate need items

You will need to purchase your immediate need items. This will include replacement of the lost or damaged clothes, household necessities and tools to help you begin your rebuilding process. This includes things like throw away clothing that you can wear when you go through the rubble. Trust me; you will never want to keep that clothing. This includes anything from cheap boots, gloves to overalls.

You will need the items when you get to "semi" permanent housing - an air mattress and sheets so that you have a place to sleep when move into your rental property. This is where all the little things come into play. Things like towels, toilet paper, toiletries, shower curtain, cooler, etc.

Kitchenware is another item to replace. Don't get me wrong you will need the right spoon for everything, but the basics are necessary in the beginning. One thing to add here is that you should get things that you enjoy and will be worth keeping. Keep the receipts for everything because you will be sending or faxing them to insurance to be reimbursed. These things will be what you repopulate your future house with.

You may get some stuff back after the fire - like Pyrex measuring cups. But you have to wait until insurance inventories everything. Then restoration people come in, pack it all up, clean it and give it back to you after several months. Most stuff will not be returned to you since they are not allowed to give you back electronic things and regular glass has a tendency to break after being in such high heat.

Keep receipts for groceries and restaurants as well. They pay you back for groceries - up to what they estimate you had in your house. They will give you a percentage of restaurant bills back until you live in your more permanent housing. Go out to a nice restaurant even if you don't feel like it. It will make you feel better. Make sure you have a few drinks if that helps you.

Keep track of your expenses and receipts

Keep track of your expenses and time in cleaning up. Keep all receipts from cleaning supplies, rental equipment and any cleaning firms you hire. Record the number of hours you and your family or friends spend cleaning up the property each day. These records will be useful if you are making an insurance claim or applying for disaster financial assistance.

6 The Claim

Remember You are the Boss

The next step is the single most important part in the process. You will need to build your team, do that effective you have understand the roles of the players.

1. <u>You are the boss</u>. You are the only person on the team looking out for your interests.
2. <u>Your insurance agent</u>. The role of the insurance agent is to be your conduit to the insurance company. The company will send all claims checks through your agent.
3. <u>The insurance company adjuster.</u> This person either works for the insurance company or is an independent contractor working on the behalf of the company.
4. <u>The housing agent</u> that works on behalf of the insurance company to provide temporary housing.
5. <u>The general contractor</u> that submits bids for the reconstruction of the property based on the adjustor's estimate. The general contracting company may perform all work itself or sub-contract to various trades.
6. <u>Other contractors</u> make the balance of the team is determined by the type of loss you have.
   a. The <u>personal property restoration contractor</u> - this is company to goes through your house after the adjuster has finished the estimate. This company will salvage what can be saved of your property, clean it up and store until you are back in your home.
   b. The <u>laundry contractor</u> - this company will attempt salvage any clothing take can be recovery, will provide a list of what could not be recovered, clean the clothing and store until you are back in your home.
   c. The <u>clean out contractor</u> - this company will remove all of the pre-construction debris from the property .
7. The <u>player to be named later</u> - this person can be your secret weapon

Meeting the Adjuster

Your insurance company will probably arrange for an adjuster to come and inspect your home. Nothing makes an adjuster happier than to be able to pay everything it takes to repair your home and satisfy you. But keep in mind the adjuster is employed by the insurance company. The adjuster first responsibility is to the insurance company.

It is very important, that this visit to home does not include any contractors or vendors. You want the complete attention of the adjuster. This will allow you to develop a relationship with adjuster. The adjuster is your interface with the insurance company.

As you work through the property surveying the damage, mention both structural and content damage. Take as much time as you need to carefully review everything. The adjuster will likely document the losses photographically.

The adjuster will offer suggestions of service providers – you are not under any obligation to accept these suggestions. Take time before making these decisions. Before letting the adjuster leave, make mention of temporary housing needs and request an advance from insurance company to handle your immediate out of pocket expenses.

Get an Advance

If you were forced to evacuate, you might not have grabbed basic necessities—from a toothbrush to clothes that you can wear to work. Your homeowner's policy will cover the cost to replace these items. Ask your company for an advance against your eventual claim. Ask a representative of the company to bring a check to you wherever you're staying, be it a hotel or a friend's house. Save the receipts for everything you buy, and be reasonable.

While waiting for the adjusters report – take you own inventory of your personal property

Remember this is your property. You document all of your property. This will be easy if you had taken an inventory prior to the fire. If not, this task will take some time. Break this task into two parts, personal property inventory and structural inventory

For a complete inventory, I recommend the following tools:
- Clothing that can be thrown away
- Gloves, safety glasses and boots
- Portable generator and lighting – this is an important investment
- Video recorder – this is an important investment
- Tape measure

Begin in one corner of the house and walk through every room, whether damaged or not, documenting the contents in extreme detail. The video camera will be a great help in this regard.

For example, I began in my living room and worked my way around the room clock wise. I described every piece of furniture, wall or window covering, photo, knickknack, linen, everything, for the video camera. I opened every concealed area and recorded the contents. This aided in completing my personal inventory. If I knew when the item was purchased and the cost, I recorded that information. Also indicating whether I considered the item damaged.

I continued from room to room and including every cabinet and closet. By the way, don't forget the basement. My last stop was the kitchen. Here I opened every cabinet and drawer documenting everything.

I then proceeded to garage and the outside of the house. Once again I documented every piece of personal property – damaged or not.

After documenting personal property, I repeated the walk-through, now concentrating on the structure itself. It is a good idea to have someone help you with this part it makes taking dimensions a little easier. Following the same process, I worked from room to room.

Beginning in the living room, I took the basic room, door, window and any other opening dimensions. In my living room, there was a built-in shelf unit. I recorded the depth, height and width of the unit and depth, height and width of the shelves.

I also recorded the location of each electrical switch, outlet (noting whether 120 or 220 volts) and fixture as well the location of size of HVAC ducts and returns.

Next I recorded the opening direction of each doorway and the type on lockset on the door. This proved to be crucial as the builder eliminated the doorway to the basement, making it a simple opening to the stairwell.

I failed to record the depth of the shelves in each of the closets and ended up with 10 inch deep shelves instead of 18 inch deep. Do not the same mistake and assume that there is a standard. This also applies to the shelve depth in the kitchen cabinets. I failed to measure these as well and now have noticeably less shelve space.

Document the results of the property inventory.

Create of list of your personal property, the appendix contains the very good template. Fill this out as completely as possible. Once complete, perform your walk-through again to make certain noting is omitted.

Dealing with the Insurance company - know your rights

You are expected to cooperate with your insurance company in respect to information requested that id related to your claim. Don't be intimidated. If you are uncomfortable answering the questions, you may want to contact an attorney before providing any information. Insurance companies are required to handle claims in a timely manner. In some states, they must send you a "notice of intentions" within 30 days of receiving your claim. If there's no dispute, you're entitled to payment within that time, too. If you haven't heard from your company and you feel that they are unnecessarily dragging their heels, write to them (and consider sending a copy to your state's Department of Insurance). Insurance companies are less likely to string you along when they're in the midst of a disaster and know that all eyes are on them.

Read everything your insurance company gives you

Sounds simple enough, right? It is, but you need to make certain you understand everything. Don't let it intimidate you. Take your time and read over it paragraph by paragraph if you have to Read it again. If something does not make sense, ask, and if it still does not make sense, seek counsel. Once you sign a document, you cannot un-sign it.

Have all claims checks delivered to you

Request that all checks be sent directly to you. Normally, these checks would require your signature as well as the contractor or vendor's for the company to cash it.

Don't let anyone rush you.

Take time and think out all your options. While documenting your loss take your time to figure up the value of all your property. When thinking about the value remember that there is a difference between "sentimental, but replaceable" and "irreplaceable." Replaceable is the furniture in your living room. Irreplaceable is frame of photos of your grandparents taken during their visit for your 5th birthday. Fight for the irreplaceable first. The replaceable is much easier to salvage and the clean-up company will try to get you to agree to let the rest go. Remember you are the boss. Don't take the first or second "No". There it is perfectly acceptable for you to get a second opinion.

Know the difference between actual cost value and replacement cost value.

This was discussed previously in the context of protecting your property. Actual Cash Value (ACV) is defined as Fair Market Value, which is the amount a willing buyer would pay a willing seller for the items. ACV does not mean replacement cost value (RCV) minus depreciation. You need to fight to get the full amounts that you are entitled to. This concept often is easily misunderstood. Your insurer ma exploit your confusion on this issue and inconsistently calculate and deduct depreciation. Seek counsel if you need help.

The ACV versus RCV discussion applies to your house as well.

Be cautious about rebuilding your home, remember, you are entitled to "Like kind and quality" Guaranteed or extended replacement cost coverage entitles you to rebuild the same quality and style home you had, even if the cost exceeds your policy limits. If the insurer say you don't have this coverage, review your policy carefully, contact the agent through whom you bought the policy and get professional help.

Always get your own estimates

You don't have to accept the insurance company's contractors. Beware of "lowball" estimates from insurance friendly contractors. You should get multiple written estimates of the true cost of replacing or repairing your home the contractor's you would hire to do the actual work.

Agree on scope

Get a "scope" of work from your adjuster that defines the amount and nature of repairs they believe are needed. Have an independent professional review and if necessary, revise the scope. Try and reach an agreement with the adjuster on a scope, then get estimates on that scope so you and the insurer are comparing "apples to apples." This resolves the most common problem that turns claims into disputes.

It's not over until you say so

Your insurance company will want to close your claim as soon as possible. The longer it's open, the greater the chance that you'll discover and file a claim for an additional loss. But homeowners often discover losses that they initially overlooked, perhaps because of the stress of living through the disaster. Protect against this possibility by waiting at least a few months before allowing your claim to be closed. You may even receive a check from the insurance company saying that you're accepting the payment "in full release of" your claim. This a common practice, don't believe it or cash it. Write Void on the check and send a copy to the insurance company along with a letter thanking the check and tell them that you do not consider the matter to be closed.

Get professional help if you need it.

Particularly on large claims, you may need the help of a professional to recover your full insurance benefits. Attorneys who specialize in representing policyholders, (insureds), and public adjusters are available and may approach you. Contingent and percentage fee agreements allow consumers economical access to professional help but affect the amount of your settlement. Percentage fees are always negotiable. Check references and professional standing.

7 Getting Help

The player to be named later.
There are three types of professionals the you can go to help with your claim.
    Public Adjuster
    Home Property Inventory professional
    Home Fire Damage Consultant

Public Adjuster
Are concerned that your insurance company isn't moving as fast with that claim check as you'd like? Or maybe the adjuster's offer is less than you need to cover your losses? Perhaps you need your own adjuster who has no relationship with your insurance company. This type of adjuster is known as public adjusters. Public Adjusters charge for their services whereas the adjuster hired by your insurance company is paid by your insurance company. Public Adjusters may charge as much 15 percent of the total value or your settlement for their services.

Public adjusters assume all of the duties necessary to have your claim processed, including making an inventory of the loss and presenting your case to the insurance company. A good public adjuster has experience in the industry and will understand your contract and the company's responsibilities right down to the fine print. In exchange, a public adjuster receives a percentage of your claim.

A Public Adjuster can perform the following tasks:
- Inspect the damaged areas with noting any and all damage that could possibly be included in the claim.
- Diagrams the affected areas to ensure accurate damage estimation.
- Document the damage to the structure and personal property using photos or video to capture the damage.
- Review the your insurance policy to be certain every coverage is being satisfied.
- Review the insurance company's estimate of damage, making note that all of the damage or the cost to replace the damaged items is correct.
- Respond to all of the correspondence with your insurance company.
- Formulate a complete estimate of damages and submit it to your insurance company along with all relevant photos for the insurance company to review.
- Meets the insurance companies claims adjuster on site at the claim to point out and negotiate any differences.

Considerations before hiring a Public Adjuster.

- Before hiring an adjuster, you should do a background check.
- Check with your state's insurance department about the licensing requirements for your state.
- Confirm that the adjuster's license is in good standing. Be wary of a copy of a license with any date other than the current year,
- Ask if and confirm that the adjuster is insured and bonded. They will be around your property.
- Check with your local Better Business Bureau for any complaints.
- Ask for at least 5 references from clients that had similar claims as yours.
- Ask to review the adjuster's contract before any work begins. Read carefully for any clauses related to mediation and any limitations as your right to speak about the service your received.
- Make certain the contract specifies exactly what fee you will be responsible for.

Home Inventory Specialist
While having home inventory before your fie is the ideal solution. Many, if not most, people don't have any documentation about their personal property. Hiring a home inventory after the fact may still be a good idea. Your insurance company's adjuster will document your damaged or destroyed property. Your personal property restoration contractor will pack up and store your belonging, but they may not provide you a list of what have collected.

Contracting with a home inventory specialist after your loss is a good idea if you don't have the time or desire to go trudging through your damaged home collecting an inventory of the your personal property. You need to have your inventory completed before any activity starts in your home. I remember doing the inventory of my home after our fire, the smell of smoke and soot permeated every corner of the house. Even in the areas not damaged by the flames.

Considerations before hiring a Home Inventory Specialist.
- Before hiring an home inventory specialist, you should do a background check.
- Check with your state's business department about the any licensing requirements.
- If required, confirm that the home inventory specialist's business license is in good standing. Be wary of a copy of a license with any date other than the current year,
- Ask if and confirm that the home inventory specialist is insured and bonded. They will be around your property.
- Check with your local Better Business Bureau for any complaints.
- Ask for references from clients that had similar claims as yours.
- Ask to review the home inventory specialist's contract before any work begins. Read carefully for any clauses related to mediation and any limitations as your right to speak about the service your received.
- Be wary if the home inventory specialist doesn't offer a contract and fee schedule before working for you.

The home inventory specialist may charge an hourly fee and a package price. Be alert that post fire, rates will be higher due to the precautions that will need to be taken working around and through debris and building materials.

Home Fire Damage Consultant
A home fire damage consultant specializes in assisting you in your property damage recovery. The

services offered by home fire damage consultant can include:

- Step by step review of the claim process.
- Review of adjuster's repair estimate to make certain that nothing is missed.
- Comparison of your home inventory to the adjuster's personal property replacement estimate.
- Comparison of your home inventory to the property restoration contractors list of your damaged and stored property.
- Reconciliation of the adjuster's estimate to your contractor's reconstruction quote.
- Secondary inspection of your home after debris and damaged building materials removal. This may expose additional damage not included in the original adjuster's estimate.
- Construction oversight and project management.
- Helping you through the process of choosing customize replacement options
- Evaluate and detail options to improve the quality if your home.
- Post completion inspection and reconciliation to the construction estimate.
- Provide assistance with the post completion punch list.
- Inspection of personal property that was restored or replaced.

I was not able to locate a home fire damage consultant to work with me. These are all steps that I took during the restoration of my home after the fire. I found the process to extremely time consuming and exhausting. The remainder of this book outlines how you can be your own home fire damage consultant.

8 Customize, Design, Exchange and Refund

The work begins
There are three ways that you can optimize rebuilding of your home.
    Customization
    Design Changes
    Exchanges
    Refunds

Customization
Once you are completed the reconciliation between the adjusters report and the contractors estimate, you should image what you want your home to look like. There are many more customizable items than just paint colors and flooring. Your contractor will likely choose the cheapest replacement items if you don't take charge. Remember you are the boss, this is your home and you are not obligated to accept the contractor's choice.

Take the contractors estimate and review each room for items you can customize to your style. Make list of these items and think about how you want your home to look. A list of these items follows:

Attic fan	Exhaust Fan	Lockset with deadbolt - Exterior
Bath - tile	Faucets	Lockset with deadbolt - Interior
Bi - fold Double Door	Flooring - Granite	Paint - Cabinet
Cabinetry	Flooring - Marble	Paint - Ceiling
Cabinetry - Hardware	Flooring - Paint	Paint - Exterior
Carpet	Flooring - Tile	Paint - Trim
Carpet - Pad	Flooring - Vinyl	Paint - Wall
Ceiling Fan	Flooring - Wood	Paneling
Countertop	Garage Door - Unit - Windows	Range Hood
Dishwasher	Garage Door - Unit & Hardware	Sink
Door - Chime	Garage Keyless Entry Pad	Smoke detector
Door - Entry - High Quality	Garage Remote Control	Thermostat
Door - Exterior - Patio	Garbage Disposal	Wallpaper
Door - Fire Rated	Garage Door Opener	Wallpaper - Border
Door - Interior	Light - switches	Window - Motorized Shades
Drapery Hardware	Light Fixture - Interior	Window - Shutter - Interior
Electrical Outlets w/ covers	Light Fixture - Exterior	Window - Blinds

This is no means an exhaustive list, your home may have other items. Thoroughly review the contractor's estimate and identify anything else that is customizable. We made some of our choices and selections at a local Home Depot store. The following list details those:

Item	RCV	Cost	Item #	Notes
Door - Exterior HG	447.50	499.00	459-547	36"
Door - Interior	166.35	63.99	769-966	24 "
Door knob - Interior	43.23	14.87	799-122	
Light Fixture HG	137.77	69.97	115-429	Minka Lavery 2 Light Model 08057
Lockset Deadbolt Ext	112.23	49.47	418-603	
Storm Door HG	244.25	209.00	205-124	EMCO 36 In. Width, Hardware Model 21104
Door - Exterior	222.33	169.00	827-425	32 ''
Light Fixture - Porcelain	26.34	5.41	358-303	Cordelia Lighting Fixture Model 4760-WH
Lock set dead bolt	80.05	49.47	418-603	
Window blind	90.78	15.97	728-766	31 x 45
Window blind Door	90.78	9.97	723-291	25 x 40
Attic Fan Whole House	524.60	369.00	221-621	
Door Chime	101.31	29.99	176-006	Heath Zenith Off-White Wireless Doorbell
Light Fixture	56.39	56.64	115-372	Minka Lavery 2 Light Model 08058
Exhaust Fan	155.86	49.83	126-831	NuTone Model 9417DN
Window Blind	90.78	8.47	171-337	23 x 48 - actual height 27
Ceiling fan	230.49	159.00	184-201	52 " Veranda
Recessed light	95.06	29.82	583-674	Hampton Bay Model EC1290WH
Sink Double	306.61	229.00	291.655	Black
Sink Faucet	147.26	159.00	316.825	
Window - Shutter	245.97	89.84	100056045	(2) Plantation Shutters Model PW1047
Bifold double Door set	189.80	57.00	418-746	(2) Model 327151
Light Fixture - Porcelain	26.34	5.41	358-303	Cordelia Lighting Model 4760-WH
Ceiling fan	230.49	159.00	761-512	52 " Ansley
Chair Rail	2.63	1.24	539-333	WM390 Solid Pine Chair Rail Model 390-LF
Door - Exterior	222.33	129.00	827-621	32 ''
Door - Interior	166.35	76.99	770-113	JELD-WEN Model 010136
Door knob - Interior	43.23	14.87	799-122	
Heat/AC Register Floor	20.46	10.98	136-120	Plated Brass Floor Register- Antique
Ceiling fan	230.49	149.00	845-679	52" Cobalt Blue
Exhaust Fan	155.86	49.83	126-831	NuTone 9417DN
Ceiling fan	230.49	179.00	560-084	54" Hampton Bay 5 blade
Light Fixture - Closet	26.34	5.41	358-303	Cordelia Lighting Model 4760-WH
Window Blind	90.78	14.47	364-283	cut to 35x44
Window Blind	90.78	15.97	365-236	cut to 29 x 20 (2)
Door Interior	166.35	66.99	769-982	JELD-WEN 30 In. x 80 In. Model 009428
Light Fixture	56.39	20.00	270-614	Change to ceiling fan

Light Fixture - Closet	26.34	5.41	358-303	Cordelia Lighting Model 4760-WH
Light Fixture	56.39	29.97	130-414	Lithonia Lighting Model FM22 ACKR LP R4
Carpet				Marion Oaks 07 SageBrush
Ceiling fan HG	360.46	229.00	926-906	56" Antigua

By making custom choices of quality items we were able to reduce the RCV expenditures by $2,451.99.

Design Changes
Depending upon the amount of damage to your home, you have the right to make any design changes that you want. Have you ever wanted to:

    change to an open floor plan
    add an island in the kitchen
    convert your master bedroom to a master suite
    convert an extra bedroom into a study or library

These possibilities can come to fruition and many can be made with little or no additional cost you. You can work with your contractor to get estimate for the changes. Additionally, cost savings can be used for any other project around house, i.e. deck, privacy fencing or landscaping.

Exchanges
Exchanges are the most promising part of the remodel. Are there features in your house to you don't like or want? Are there features you want to add. The following list contains some of the exchanges we made during our remodel:

Exchange	Value	Add Description	Contractor	Owner
Garage - Paneling	630.00			
Garage - Pegboard	50.88			
Garage – Shelving	76.27			
Garage – Gas Heater	930.26			
Sitting Room – Baseboard heater	1051.88	Sitting Room – HVAC Venting	975.00	
Sitting Room – Fan / Light	198.00	Sitting Room – Ceiling Fan / Light	125.00	
Sitting Room - Wallpaper	372.07	Sitting Room - paint	375.00	
Sitting Room – Window Covering	843.37	Self-purchased		412.00
Kitchen – Appliances - Dishwasher	298.00	Self-purchased		499.00
Kitchen – Appliances - Range	932.58	Self-purchased		699.00
Kitchen – Appliances – Range Hood	249.00	Self-purchased – Microwave		299.00
Kitchen – Appliances - Refrigerator				1010.52
Kitchen – Fluorescent Light	57.56	Kitchen – Ceiling fan / Light	125.00	
Kitchen - Paneling	937.78			
Kitchen - Wallpaper	460.63			
Kitchen – Wood Shutters	484.74			
Kitchen – Window Blinds	239.95	Self-purchased / installed		120.00
Office - Wallpaper Border	145.20			
Office – Window Blind	169.94	Self-purchased / installed		80.00
Bedroom - Wallpaper Border	145.20			

Bedroom – Window Blinds	169.94	Self-purchased / installed		80.00
Master Bedroom - Wallpaper Border	145.20			
Master Bedroom – Window Blinds	169.94	Self-purchased / installed		80.00
Hall – High Grade Thermostat	142.84	Self-purchased / installed		249.00
Exchange Sub Total	8,901.23		1,600.00	3,528.52

To figure the net benefit, subtract the contractor add cost from the exchange subtotal:

$$8901.23 - 1600.00 = 7301.23$$

Add the profit and overhead margins of 10% each

$$\text{Multiply } 7301.23 \text{ by } 1.2 = 8761.47$$

Subtract the cost of the self-purchased items:

$$8761.47 - 3828.52 = 5232.96$$

That is additional $5,232.96 into your pocket.

Refunds

One last thing and potentially most important task reconcile the contractor's estimate to the work actually completed. This is also known as the punch list. The best approach is to look at this as a home inspection. If you don't feel comfortable performing this task you can hire a professional to do this for you.

The easiest approach is to take the contractor's estimate and go room by room checking off the items that have been completed. Also you have to look at the items that are not easily visible, while being a challenge, this is very important. The following is the punch list I created for our house.

Line Item	DESCRIPTION	Labor	Material	Equipment	Market Condition	Total	Refund
32	Clean with pressure/chemical spray - Heavy	76.84	4.27	29.88	0.00	136.60	136.60
177 b	Clothes dryer vent - installed	3.03	24.86	0.00	0.00	46.78	46.78
233	Seal & paint vanity - inside and out	17.68	14.96	0.00	0.00	89.88	89.88
292	Seal & paint wood shelving, 12"- 24" width	20.16	15.84	0	0	100.80	100.80
383	Seal then paint the walls and ceiling (2 coats)	103.09	123.71	0.00	226.82	804.13	804.13
409	Paint door slab only - 2 coats (per side)	6.20	9.36	0.00	0.02	35.70	35.70
410	Paint door/window trim & jamb – 2 coats (per side)	7.16	5.68	0.00	0.00	36.06	36.06
431 b	Flashing - pipe jack	5.20	12.40	0.00	0.00	39.16	39.16
435 b	Furnace vent - rain cap and storm collar, 6"	2.18	25.13	0.00	0.00	40.89	40.89
440	Clean with pressure / chemical spray	28.04	7.01	28.04	0.00	147.21	147.21
441	Exterior - Paint two coats	84.12	133.19	0.00	0.00	497.71	497.71
455	Soffit vent	18.84	18.00	0.00	12.52	129.36	129.36
457	Clean with pressure/chemical spray (Note: power wash driveway upon completion of repairs.)	20.00	5.00	20.00	0.00	105.00	105.00
462	Clean with pressure/chemical spray	9.12	2.28	9.12	0.00	47.88	47.88
475	Clean with pressure/chemical spray	26.32	6.58	26.32	0.00	138.18	138.18
476	Exterior - paint two coats	78.96	125.02	0.00	0.00	467.18	467.18

486	Soffit vent	18.84	18.00	0.00	12.52	129.36	129.36
488 b	Attic vent - gable end - metal - 30" x 30"	14.14	100.00	0.00	0.00	174.14	174.14
490	Clean with pressure/chemical spray	17.24	4.31	17.24	0.00	90.51	90.51
491	Exterior - paint two coats	51.72	81.89	0.00	0.00	306.01	306.01
498	Soffit vent	18.84	18.00	0.00	12.52	129.36	129.36
507 b	Blown-in insulation - 14" depth - R38	117.74	1177.35	78.49	0.00	2001.50	
508	Insulation Installer - per hour Note: Additional labor for difficult attic access on low pitch roof.	16.66	0.00	0.00	0.00	103.60	
512	Clean ductwork - Interior (PER REGISTER)	44.00	315.00	0.00	0.00	504.80	

We had the contractor arrange to complete the insulation installation and the cleaning of the duct. We elected to seek refunds from the contractors for the majority of the items dealing with the house's exterior. The refund of $4,210.32 (including the credit for overhead and profit) was used to hire our own painter to properly paint the exterior. After painting we replaced all of the soffit and attic vents that the contractor failed to install.

The contractor was trying to make up time to get use back into our home on schedule. Several omissions would be understandable. The lack of proper exterior repainting was inexcusable.

Through our involvement in the rebuilding process we reduced the payable to the contractor in total of $11,195.55.

APPENDIX

APPENDIX 1

Glossary of Relevant terms

Abandonment Clause: A clause often contained in property insurance policies stating that the insured cannot abandon damaged property to the insurer and demand to be reimbursed for its full value

Accident: A fortuitous, unexpected, unintended event occurring suddenly.

Act of God: A natural disaster or force of nature, such as an earthquake, hurricane or flood.

Actual Cash Value (ACV): The cost to replace an item of property at the time of loss, less an allowance for depreciation. Often used to determine amount of reimbursement for a loss (Replacement Cost ? Depreciation).

Additional insured: This is an individual, company or some other entity that is not considered the insured as defined under the insurance policy of another, but may be added to that policy by endorsement to afford a degree of insurance protection.

Adjuster: A representative of the insurer who arranges for adjustment and/or settlement of a loss

Additional Living Expenses: A provision in many policies to provide reimbursement for costs above the normal living expenses, incurred because the insured is forced to live away from home while the home is being repaired because of fire or other damage. It applies to such expenses as restaurant meals, hotel rooms, transportation etc. The company, however, is bound only to pay to maintain the insured's usual standard of living.

Agent: Usually an insurance company appointed representative which is licensed by the state in which they do business. They can solicit, market, negotiate, bind, and administer insurance policies for the insurer.

Aggregate Limit: A type of policy limit found in liability policies which limits coverage to a specified total amount for all losses occurring within the policy period.

Agreed value: An agreement between the insurer and the insured that the limit of insurance on a scheduled item of property equals the property's value. For some items, such as jewelry and fine arts, the insurer may require an appraisal.

All Risk Insurance: Insurance protecting the insured from loss arising from any peril other than those perils specifically excluded by name. This contrasts with Named Peril insurance, which names the peril or perils insured against.

Allied Lines: Property coverage's which are closely associated and frequently sold with fire insurance: Dwelling insurance, Earthquake insurance, Sprinkler Leakage, etc.

Application: Form to collect information for a particular account.

Appraisal: A survey of values in order to determine the appropriate amount of insurance to be written or the proper amount of loss to be paid.

Appraisal Clause: A property insurance policy provision that allows an insured and insurer who cannot reach an agreement on the amount of a loss settlement to each select their own appraiser. The appraisers then select a neutral umpire. Disagreements between the appraisers are settled by the umpire, whose decisions are usually binding on both parties.

Assignment: Transfer of a legal right or interest in a policy from one party to another (as when an insured property is sold).

Assignment Clause: A condition in insurance policies that specifies that transferring the policy to another is not valid unless the company consents to it in writing.

Bind: The agent or company representative agrees to cover the item/person etc. until the formal insurance contract is issued.

Binder: An oral or written statement providing immediate insurance protection, valid for a specified period. Designed to provide temporary coverage until a policy can be issued or denied.

Binding Authority: Authority granted by the insurance company who will ultimately assume responsibility for providing coverage. Allows an agent to act on behalf of the company for specific reasons and within prescribed guidelines.

Broker: One who represents an insured in the solicitation, negotiation, or placement of insurance.

Broker of Record: A common term of "Agent of Record" is used to designate the broker who is to handle certain insurance policies for the named insured

Cancellation: Termination of an insurance policy in force by a voluntary act of the insured or by insurer for lack of payment, fraud, misrepresentation etc.

Captive Agent: An agent under exclusive contract to one company.

Catastrophe: An event which loss is of extraordinary magnitude, such as a hurricane or tornado

Certificate of Insurance: Evidence to another that one has insurance of a certain type and amount. Proof of insurance.

Civil commotion: A general disturbance or uprising of a number of people who threaten or commit acts of violence and destroy property. Civil commotion is an insurable peril under most property insurance policies and is fundamentally the same as riot.

Claim: The assertion of a legal right against an insurer that carries with it a demand for appropriate relief.

Collapse: To fall down or inward; the abrupt failure or imminent fundamental weakening of a wall or foundation of a structure. Collapse is covered in most property policies when it is due to an insured peril. Collapse does not include settling, cracking, shrinkage, bulging or expansion.

Concealment: The withholding of a material fact from the insurance company. May void the policy.

Concurrent Insurance: Two or more policies with the same conditions that cover the same interest in identical property.

Conditions: The portion of an insurance contract which sets forth the rights and duties of the insured and the insurance company.

Consequential Damage: Damage which occurs as "consequence" of a direct loss, such as loss from spoilage resulting from lack of power, light, heat, etc. Not generally covered under property policies unless specified.

Consequential Loss: A loss arising indirectly from an insured peril, such as damage to goods as a result of fire that causes failure of refrigeration while not actually burning the stored goods themselves.

Constructive total loss: Damage to property that does not totally destroy it but renders it valueless to the insured or prevents it from being restored to the original condition except at a cost exceeding its value; therefore, it is deemed a total loss.

Contract: A legal agreement between two parties promising a certain performance in exchange for a certain consideration.

Debris removal clause: Insurance coverage for the expense of removing debris that results from a loss covered by the policy if the limit of insurance is insufficient to cover both the amount of direct loss and the added cleanup. Many property policies provide an additional $5,000 for each insured location. Higher limits must be purchased separately.

Declarations: The page of an insurance contract that indicates the name of the policyholder, the insurance company, the period of coverage, what is covered (property, liability) under the contract.

Declination: Rejection of an application for insurance by the insurer.

Deductible: Usually, a dollar amount the insured must pay on each loss to which the deductible applies. The insurance company pays the remainder of each covered loss up to the policy limits. See also Franchise, Percentage and Straight.

Depreciation: Decrease in the value of any type of tangible property over a period of time resulting from use, wear and tear and obsolescence.

Documentation: Supporting evidence or proof as to what has been done and the reason therefore.

Domestic Insurer: An insurance company formed under the laws of the state in which the insurance is written.

Draft: A form of payment, almost like a check.

Draft Authority: Authority granted to the agent by the insurance company to handle small claims and issue drafts within prescribed limits.

Dwelling Policy: An allied lines policy which provides coverage for the dwellings and personal property of individuals and families against fire and additional perils.

Effective Date: The beginning of the policy term, usually 12:01 a.m. of the date shown.

Endorsement: A document which is attached to the policy and modifies or changes the original policy in some way.

Equal Shares Clause: An insurance clause which states that when the insured has other insurance, the loss payment made by the company will be based on the number of applicable policies, not on their limits.

Exclusions: Section of the insurance policy which lists property, perils, persons, or situations which are not covered under the policy.

Expiration Date: The date that coverage ceases to be provided by an insurance policy.

Exposure: The state of being subject to the possibility of loss.

Fair Market Value: The price that a willing buyer would pay and a willing seller would accept in an arm's length transaction in a competitive (i.e., not monopolistic) market. Same as Market Value.

Fire: Combustion accompanied by a flame or glow, which escapes normal confines to cause damage

First Party Insurance: A loss which applies to the insured's own property or person and thus involves only the insurer and the insured.

Form: An insurance document such as a policy, endorsement, rider or application.

Hazard: Something that increases the chance of loss. For instance, faulty wiring is a hazard because it increases the chance of a fire loss.

Hold Harmless Agreement: A contractual arrangement whereby one party assumes the liability in a given situation, thereby relieving the other party of responsibility.

Homeowners Policy: A personal multiple line contract incorporating both property and liability coverages. Several different forms provide varying degrees of protection.

Indemnity: A principle of insurance which provides that when a loss occurs, the insured should be restored to the approximate financial condition occupied before the loss occurred, no better, no worse.

Independent Insurance Agent: One who represents more than one company, sells and services the insurance solely on a commission or fee basis under contract, and is recognized to own the business produced.

Indirect Damage: Loss resulting as a consequence of physical damage to property.

Indirect Loss: Loss which is a result or consequence of a direct loss.

Inflation Guard: A property insurance option which provides that the policy limits will increase a certain percentage at regular intervals, for instance, annually.

Insurable Interest: Any actual, lawful and substantial economic interest in the safety or preservation of the subject of the insurance from loss, destruction or pecuniary damage or impairment. A claim may be paid only when an insurable interest exists.

Insurance: A contract whereby one undertakes to indemnify another or pay or allow a specified amount or a determinable benefit upon determinable contingencies.

Insurance to value: Insurance coverage written at or near the value of the insured property; or the ratio that the amount of the insurance purchased bears to the value of the insured property.

Insured: Also referred to as the policyholder. The person, business or other entity that is covered by the policy.

Insured peril: The danger to a property against which it is insured; a cause of loss that invokes coverage under a policy. For example, fire, explosion, wind and vandalism are insured perils under a typical property insurance policy.

Insurer: The insurance company.

Insuring Agreement: The section of an insurance policy which states which losses will be indemnified, what property is covered, which perils are insured against.

Lapse: A policy becoming invalid because of failure to pay the premium on time.

Limits of Liability: The maximum amount of insurance the insurance company will pay for a particular loss, or for a loss during a period of time.

Loss: The reduction in value of the insured's property, the amount sought in his claim or the amount paid under a liability policy.

Loss of Use Coverage: Under the Homeowners contract, covers the insured's increased cost of living after loss and rental value of any portion of the dwelling which is rented out.

Misrepresentation: Statement of something that is known to be untrue.

Mortgagee: One who has a lender's interest in real property.

Mortgagee clause: An endorsement attached to a fire or other direct damage policy that covers mortgaged property, specifying that the loss reimbursement will be paid to the mortgagee as the mortgagee's interest may appear; that the mortgagee's rights of recovery will not be defeated by any act or neglect of the insured; and giving the mortgagee other rights, privileges, and duties.

Mortgagor: One who has secured a loan from a mortgagee, usually the property owner, and thus the insured under a property policy.

Named Insured: Any person, firm, or corporation designated by name as the specific insured in a policy.

Named Perils Policy: A policy specifying only those perils to be insured against, in contrast to a policy that insures all perils not specifically excluded.

Negligence: The failure to exercise that degree of care that the law requires to protect others from an unreasonable risk of harm. The failure to act as a prudent person would have acted under similar circumstances.

Occupancy: The type and character of the use of the property and the entity therein.

Percentage Deductible: A deductible which requires a deduction from the loss of a percentage of the value of the property.

Peril: The cause of loss. Examples include fire, windstorm or explosion.

Personal property: Property other than real estate, or property that is movable or separable from real estate; for property insurance purposes, tangible property, which is often called "contents." Personal property may be used for business purposes and therefore may be covered by a commercial policy, while personal property not used for business purposes is generally covered only by personal lines policies (such as homeowners or renters' insurance).

Policy: An insurance contract.

Policy Period: The period during which the policy contract is in force and affords protection, from inception date to expiration date.

Premises: The particular location of property as designated in the policy.

Premium: The consideration (price) paid by the insured to the insurer for insurance protection over a specified period.

Premium Finance: Allows the insured to pay part of the premium when coverage takes effect and pay the rest during the policy period through arranged payments.

Preservation of Property: This is a property insurance coverage, sometimes known as a removal, which provides coverage for property that has been removed from the premises to protect it following a covered loss.

Primary Insurance: When two or more coverages or policies apply to the same loss, the one which pays first, up to its limit of liability or the amount of the loss, whichever is less. See excess insurance.

Proof Of Loss: The evidence offered by the insured to prove entitlement to collect the amount claimed from the insurer or the statement, signed and sworn by the insured, setting forth the claim information required by the policy.

Property Damage: A type of loss covered under many liability contracts. Property damage means physical injury to tangible property, including loss of use.

Property insurance: Coverage for real or personal property lost or damaged by a covered peril and, sometimes, consequential financial losses resulting from property damage. It is first-party coverage.

Proposal: A written presentation to a prospect indicating various coverages, options, and may also include premiums.

Rebate: The unlawful practice of returning a part of a premium to an insured.

Renewal: The continuation of coverage for another period after a policy has expired.

Replacement Cost: The cost to replace a damaged or destroyed item of property, without deducting depreciation. May be the basis of reimbursement for loss to buildings, or by endorsement, to personal property.

Replacement Cost Endorsement: An endorsement that can be added to an HO-3 form to provide replacement cost coverage on personal property (with limitations).

Schedule: A list of individual items covered under one policy with specific amounts of insurance applicable to each.

Scheduled Personal Property Endorsement: An endorsement to the Homeowners policy that schedules specific amounts of coverage for one or more of several categories of personal property on an all risks basis.

Settlement: An adjustment where the disposition of the claim involves the payment of a sum of money to the insured or third-party claimant.

Total Loss: The complete destruction of insured property; property that has disappeared or has been damaged irreparably or so there is no salvageable or reparable value. A total loss usually signifies the maximum settlement under the terms of a policy.

Underwriter: The insurance company or group that underwrites or insures a particular risk. It is also used as the identification of the individual within the company whose responsibility it is to accept or reject business in the particular line in which they specialize and in this way chooses risks their principals are prepared to underwrite.

Unoccupied: A building that is furnished but in which nobody resides. Some property insurance policies suspend coverage if a building is unoccupied for more than a specified time, usually 60 or 90 days.

Utmost Good Faith: A principle of insurance which states that the insurance company must be able to rely on the honesty and cooperation of the insured, and the insured must rely on the company to fulfill its obligations in good faith.

Vacancy: The absence of people and personal property from a building. Property coverage is often restricted when there are long periods of vacancy.

Warranty: A specific agreement between the insured and the insurer that certain conditions will be met. This agreement becomes a part of the policy.

Write: To insure, to underwrite or to take an application.

APPENDIX 2

Inventory Worksheets

Downloadable versions are available at https://www.from-the-ash.us/worksheets/

Appliances – Major	Qty	Description	Purchased	Cost
Built in Range				
Dishwasher				
Dryer				
Electronic air filter				
Exhaust fan/hood				
Garbage disposal				
Microwave				
Range / Stove				
Refrigerator				
Wall oven				
Washing machine				

Appliances – Small	Qty	Description	Purchased	Cost
Air Fryer				
Blender				
Bread maker				
Cappuccino/espresso maker				
Chicken fryer				
Clothes steamer				
Coffee grinder				
Coffee maker				
Coffee pot				
Crock pot/slow cooker				
Deep fryer				
Dutch oven				
Electric can opener				
Electric deep fryer				
Electric fondue pot				
Electric fry pan				
Electric griddle				
Electric grill				
Electric hand mixer				
Electric juicer				
Electric knife				
Electric knife sharpener				
Electric mixer				
Electric wok				

Appliances – Small	Qty	Description	Purchased	Cost
Fondue pot				
Food dehydrator				
Food processor				
Food sealer				
Food slicer				
Foreman Grill				
Ice cream maker				
Indoor grill				
Iron				
Mixer - hand				
Mixer - stand				
Pasta machine				
Popcorn popper				
Pressure cooker				
Sewing machine				
Toaster				
Toaster oven				
Tortilla warmer				
Trash compacter				
Waffle maker				

Notes:

Baby's room	Qty	Description	Purchased	Cost
Air conditioner (room)				
Area rugs				
Baby blankets				
Baby cloths				
Baby monitor				
Baby wipes				
Bibs/Washcloths				
Books				
Car seat				
Ceiling - ceiling fan				
Clock				
Clothes hamper				
Collapsible door guard				
Comb/Brush				
Crib/Bed sheets				
Curtains/Rods/Brackets				
Diapers				
DVDs/CDs/Videos				
Frames				
Hangers				
Hats/Socks				
Light bulbs				
Liquid soap				
Mirrors				
Mobile				
Nanny cam				
Nappies/Onesies				
Pacifier/Sippee cup				
Photos/frames				
Pictures/Frames				
Pillows/Cases				
Plants, planters				
Plastic crib liner				
Shades, blinds, curtains				
Shelving/Brackets				
Shelving/storage				
Soaps/Lotions				
Table lamp				
Telephone				
Thermometer				
Throw pillows				
Tissue				
Toy chest				

Baby's room	Qty	Description	Purchased	Cost
Vaseline				
Waste basket				

Bar	Qty	Description	Purchased	Cost
Bottle id tags				
Bottle opener				
Chalkboard/Chalk				
Clock/batteries				
Condiments/Snacks				
Curtains/Rods/Brackets				
Drink coasters				
Framed Art/Décor				
Glassware				
Ice Bucket/Tongs				
Light bulbs				
Mini-Refrigerator				
Napkins				
Plastic Cups/Plates				
Rug/Rug pad				
Serving trays				
Shaker/Strainer				
Shelving/Brackets				
Surge protector				
Swizzle/Umbrellas				
Trash Can/Bags				
Wine journal				
Wine rack				

Notes:

Bath	Qty	Description	Purchased	Cost
Air conditioner (room)				
Aloe Vera				
Bandage strips				
Bath mat				
Bath salts/Bath oils				
Bath scrub brush				
Bath soap and gels				
Bath toys				
Bathtub/Jacuzzi				
Blush				
Books or magazines				
Books/Magazines				
Candles				
Ceiling - ceiling fan				
Chairs, stuffed chairs and cushions				
Cleaning products				
Cleaning supplies				
Clock and/or clock radio				
Clothes hamper				
Combs and brushes				
Corded, handheld, handsfree				
Cosmetics				
Cotton balls/Sponges				
Cough drops				
Curling irons				
Curtains/Rods/Brackets				
Deodorant				
Drinking glass				
Elastic bandages				
Electric/Sonar toothbrush				
Eye color				
Eye concealer				
Eye drops				
Eye glasses/contacts				
Eye liner				
Feminine hygiene products				
First-aid kits				
First-aid tape/Scissors				
Foot brush/Pumice				
Foot spray				
Foundation/Toner				
Framed art/Decor				
Frames				

Bath	Qty	Description	Purchased	Cost
Gel and hair products				
Hair color				
electric rollers				
Hair dryers				
Hair pins/Barrettes				
Heating pad				
Hot water bottle				
Ice bag				
Lash curler				
Light bulbs				
Lip liner				
Lipstick/Lip gloss				
Lotions/Creams				
Make-up brushes				
Mascara				
Mirrors				
Mouthwash				
Nail files				
Nail polish/Clear coat				
Non-prescription medicines				
Ointments				
Over-counter medicine				
Perfumes/Cologne				
Photos/Frames				
Plants, planters				
Plunger				
Polish remover				
Prescription medicines				
Q-tips				
Rubbing alcohol				
Rugs				
Safety pins				
Scale				
Sconce				
Scrunches/Hair bands				
Shades, blinds, curtains				
Shampoo/Conditioner				
Shavers/Razors				
Shower				
Shower curtain				
Shower curtain rings				
Shower curtain/liner				
Sinks				
Soap dish				

Bath	Qty	Description	Purchased	Cost
Soap/Soap dish				
Sterile bandages				
Sterile cotton				
Sun block				
Tissue holder				
Toilet and bidet				
Toilet paper				
Toilet seat cover				
Toothbrush holder				
Toothbrush/Paste/Floss				
Toothbrushes				
Trimmers/Scissors				
Tweezers/Clippers				
Vanity and bench				
Washcloths				
Waste basket				
Water glass				
Weight scale				

Notes:

Bedroom	Qty	Description	Purchased	Cost
Air conditioner				
Books				
Ceiling – ceiling fan				
Chairs, stuffed chairs and cushions				
Clock and/or clock radio				
Clothes hamper				
Frames				
Hangers				
Mirrors				
Other				
Photos/Frames				
Plants, planters				
Rugs				
Sconce				
Shades, blinds, curtains				
Shelving/storage				
Sleeping pillows				
Storage				
Table				
Table Lamp				
Telephone				
Vanity and bench				
Wastebasket				

Boy's accessories / Clothing	Qty	Description	Purchased	Cost
Active wear				
Blank media disks				
Blazers				
Bracelets				
Cuff links				
Dress pants				
Earrings				
Footwear/shoes/boots/sandals				
Footwear/shoes/boots/sandals/running				
Holiday - formal occasion				
Jeans				
Necklaces				
Outerwear (coats, scarves, gloves)				
Pajamas				
Pants				
Rings				
Shirts				

Shirts (buttoned down)				
Shirts (pullover)				
Shoes/Slippers				
Shorts				
Sleepwear				
Socks/Underwear				
Suits				
Sweaters				
Swimsuit				
Ties				
Undergarments and socks				
Watches				

Child's Room	Qty	Description	Purchased	Cost
Books/Magazines				
Clock/Alarm cock				
Clothes hamper				
Clothes hangers				
Comb/Brush				
Curtains/Rods/Brackets				
Duvet/Cover				
DVDs/Videos/CDs				
Electronic gaming				
Hair ties/Barrettes				
Light bulbs				
Pictures/Frames				
Piggy bank/Coins				
Posters/Decor				
Puzzles/Games/Cards				
Quilts/Quilt holder				
Rain boots/Rain coats				
Shelving/Brackets				
Shoe organizer				
Sporting equipment				
Storage units				
Stuffed toys				
Throw pillows				
Trophies/Medals				
Waste basket				

Notes:

Décor	Qty	Description	Purchased	Cost
Accessory pillows				
Art and pictures				
Baskets				
Chairs, stuffed chairs and cushions				
Framed Art				
Frames/photos				
Globe				
Silk flowers				
Wall hangings				
Buffet				
Candles				
Candlesticks				
Center piece				
China cabinet				
China pattern				
China serving pieces				
Crystal barware				
Crystal candlesticks				
Crystal stemware				
Crystal vases				
curio				
Napkin rings				
Silver plate				
Silverware pattern				

Notes:

Electronics	Qty	Description	Purchased	Cost
All-in-One computer				
Analog TV				
Answering machine				
Blue Ray DVDs				
Blue Ray player				
Bluetooth speakers				
Cable Boxes				
Cable organizer				
Camcorder				
Camera carrying cases				
CD burner				
Cell phone				
Cell phone accessories				
Cell phone charger				
Desktop computer				
Digital media cards				
Digital readers - Kindle				
Digital camera				
DirecTV or Dish control box				
Drone				
DVD player				
DVDs				
External back-up drive				
Fax machine				
Game Systems				
Games				
HD TV				
Home assistant devices				
Home theater system				
Keyboard				
Laptop Computer				
LCD projector				
LCD TV				
Media Server				
Modems				
Monitor				
Mouse				
Mouse pad				
Music CDs				
Printer				
Radio				
Routers				
Satellite dish				

Electronics	Qty	Description	Purchased	Cost
Software				
Software media				
Sound bar				
Speakers/Speaker wire				
Stereo receiver				
Streaming media devices				
Surge protector				
Surround sound system 5.1				
Surround sound system 7.1				
Tablets - iPads				
TV stands				
TV wall mount				
UHD DVD player				
Ultra HD TV				
Universal remote control				
VCR player				
VCR Tapes				
Video Security System				
Web camera				
Wireless security cameras				
Wireless speaker				

Notes:

Entry	Qty	Description	Purchased	Cost
Books/Magazines				
Cedar moth balls				
Clothes hangers/Hooks				
Coats/Jackets				
Curtains/Rods/Brackets				
Flashlight/Batteries				
Hat tree/Hats				
Letter opener				
Light bulbs				
Mail organizer				
Other:				
Pictures/Frames				
Radio/Batteries				
Rain boots/Rain coats				
Rug/Rug pad				
Scarves/Gloves				
Shoes/Boots				
Umbrellas				
Wastebasket				

Exterior Activities	Qty	Description	Purchased	Cost
ATV				
Backpacks				
Badminton net/Rackets				
Barometer				
BBQ tools				
Benches				
Bicycles/Helmets/Gloves				
Bike trailers				
Birdfeed/Seeds				
Birdfeeder/Squirrel house				
Boat - canoe, sail, inboard, outboard				
Boat - lifejackets				
Boat - paddles, sails, motor				
Bocce balls				
Boogie boards				
Buckets/Trays				
Camping dishes				
Camping grills				
Camping sleeping bags				
Camping tarp				
Camping tent				

Exterior Activities	Qty	Description	Purchased	Cost
Candles/Candleholders				
Candles/Lanterns				
Casual flatware				
Chairs, stuffed chairs and cushions				
Chairs/Tables				
Chalk/Markers/Eraser				
Charcoal/Fire starter				
Chimes				
Chlorine tabs				
Clippers/Pruners				
Composter				
Coolers				
Corkboard/Dry erase				
Curtains/Rods/Brackets				
Drink coasters				
Exterior speakers/Wire				
Fertilizers/Bug sprays				
Fish food				
Flag/Flagpole				
Floating devices/Toys				
Food wastebasket				
Fountain/Pond				
Framed art/Decor				
Freestanding mailbox				
Garden edging				
Garden gloves				
Garden gnome				
Garden hose/Sprinkler				
Garden mirrored ball				
Garden pots and holder				
Garden seeds and bulbs				
Garden sprays				
Garden stakes				
Garden tools				
Goggles/Fins/Masks				
Grill and accessories				
Grill baskets				
Hammock and hammock stand				
Hand tools				
Holiday and outdoor décor				
Horse shoes/Stakes				
Hose nozzle sprayer				
Hoses/Hose winder				
Hot pads/Gloves				

Exterior Activities	Qty	Description	Purchased	Cost
Hot tub				
Inline skates				
Knee pads				
Lanterns				
Lawn furniture - chairs, recliners, tables				
Lawn mower (push, electric, riding)				
Lawn seed and fertilizer				
Leaf blower				
Leashes				
Light bulbs				
Matches/Fluid				
Mosquito zapper				
Outdoor chair and cushions				
Outdoor coffee table				
Outdoor ottoman and cushions				
Outdoor pillows				
Outdoor sofa and cushions				
Outdoor table				
Path lighting				
Patio lights				
Planters				
Plastic plates/Cups				
Pool floatation devices				
Potting soil				
Rakes/Hoes/Spades				
Recycling crate				
Rocking chairs				
Scrubbers/Poles/Nets				
Seat cushions				
Seeds/Plants				
Skates/Helmets/Pads				
Ski boots				
Ski hat/goggles/mittens				
Ski jackets/ski pants				
Ski poles				
Skis				
Sleds/Plastic disks				
Snow blower				
Snow shovel				
Snow sleds				
Snowmobile				
Snowshoes				
Sprinkler spare parts				
Storage containers				

Exterior Activities	Qty	Description	Purchased	Cost
Storage units				
Surfboards/Wetsuits				
Tablecloths/Napkins				
Tables				
Temperature gauge				
Tennis net/Rackets/Balls				
Towels/Bathrobes				
Trellises				
Umbrellas				
Volleyball net/Volleyball				
Wastebasket				
Water ski tow ropes				
Water skis				
Water sprinklers				
Water treatments				
Watering can/Mister				
Wheelbarrow				
Wood/Ceramic planters				
Wooden swing				

Notes:

Family room	Qty	Description	Purchased	Cost
Ashtrays/Lighters				
Books/Magazines				
Clock				
Collectibles				
Curtains/Rods/Brackets				
Drink coasters				
Encyclopedia				
Fan				
Fireplace screen				
Fireplace tools				
Floor lamp				
Flower vases				
Log holder				
Magnifying glass				
Matches/Logs				
Mirrors				
Paperweights				
Pens/Pencils/Paper				
Photo albums				
Pictures/Frames				
Rugs/Rug pads				
Wastebasket				
Window hardware				
Window treatments				

Notes:

Furniture	Qty	Description	Purchased	Cost
Armoire				
Baby crib				
Bar chairs				
Bar table				
Bed box spring - full				
Bed box spring - king				
Bed box spring - queen				
Bed box spring - twin				
Bed box spring -king				
Bed frame - full				
Bed frame - king				
Bed frame - queen				
Bed frame - twin				
Bed headboard - full				
Bed headboard - king				
Bed headboard - queen				
Bed headboard - twin				
Bed side table				
Bench				
Bench cushion				
Bookcase - 3 shelve				
Bookcase - 4 shelve				
Bookcase - 5 shelve				
Buffet				
Cabinet - free standing				
Chairs, stuffed chairs and cushions				
Cocktail table				
Coffee table				
Computer and printer stands				
Computer desk				
Couch				
Dining chairs				
Dining room table				
Dressers				
End tables				
Entertainment center				
Folding table				
Home theater seating				
Hutch				
Kitchen chairs, bar stools				
Kitchen island				
Loveseat				
Mattress - baby				

Furniture	Qty	Description	Purchased	Cost
Mattress/Foundation - full				
Mattress/Foundation - king				
Mattress/Foundation - queen				
Mattress/Foundation - twin				
Microwave table				
Office chair				
Ottoman				
Playpen				
Recliner				
Reclining sofa				
Rocker recliner				
Rocking chair				
Sofa				
Student desk				
Table				
Work desk				

Notes:

Game room	Qty	Description	Purchased	Cost
Billiards/Chalk				
Binoculars				
Board games				
Books/Magazines				
Cards/Dice/Chips				
Chess/Checkers				
Curtains/Rods/Brackets				
Darts/Dartboard				
Pictures/Frames				
Ping pong ball/Paddles				
Pool cues/Triangle				
Rug/Rug pad				
Scorecards				
Shelving/Brackets				
Sport memorabilia				

Notes:

Girl's accessories / clothing	Qty	Description	Purchased	Cost
Active wear				
Blazers				
Bracelets (wrist and ankle)				
Dress pants				
Earrings				
Footwear/shoes/boots/sandals				
Footwear/shoes/boots/sandals/running				
Holiday - formal occasion				
Jeans				
Necklaces				
Outerwear (coats, scarves, gloves)				
Pants				
Pins				
Rings				
School uniforms				
Shirts (buttoned down)				
Shirts (pullover)				
Shorts				
Skirts				
Sleepwear				
Sweaters				
Swimsuit				
Undergarments and socks				
Watches				

Guest room	Qty	Description	Purchased	Cost
Bookends				
Books/Magazines				
Clothes hamper				
Clothes hangers				
Clothes hooks				
Curtains/Rods/Brackets				
Mirror				
Rug/Rug pad				
Shelving/Brackets				
Wastebasket				

Notes:

Kitchen	Qty	Description	Purchased	Cost
Appetizer Skewers				
Aprons				
Bakeware				
Baking Trays				
Beer steins/glasses				
Books - cookbooks and notes				
Bottle openers				
Bowl set				
Bowls - cereal or pasta				
Bowls - soup				
Bread box				
Bread trays				
Broiler pan				
Broom/Pan/Mop				
Bundt cake pan				
Butter dish				
Butter knives				
Cake pans				
Cake plates				
Can opener				
Candle snuffers				
Candles				
Canister sets				
Canisters				
Carving boards				
Carving knife/fork				
Casserole set				
Ceiling - ceiling fan				
Chafing dishes				
Champagne/wine coolers				
Cheese board				
Cheese grater				
Cheese knife				
Cheese plates				
Cleaning bucket				
Cleaning supplies				
Cleaning towels				
Cleaver				
Clock				
Cloth dishtowels				
Coaster set				
Colander				
Cookbooks/Holder				

Kitchen	Qty	Description	Purchased	Cost
Cookie jar				
Cookie sheets				
Cookware				
Corkscrews				
Corn nibs				
Cream pitcher				
Cups and mugs				
Cutlery				
Cutting boards				
Dish Soap/Tray				
Dish Towels				
Double boiler				
Drink coasters				
Fire extinguisher				
Flatware				
Flower vases				
Fondue				
Frames				
Freezer				
Frying pan				
Gadgets				
Garlic press				
Gelatin molds				
Glassware				
Gravy boat				
Griddle				
Guacamole dish				
Hand can opener				
Hand grater				
Hand juicer				
Hand soap				
Hand whisks				
High ball glasses				
High tumblers				
Hot pads				
Jellyroll pans				
Juice pitcher				
Kitchen shears				
Knife block				
Knives - boning				
Knives - bread				
Knives - butcher				
Knives - carving				
Knives - paring				

Kitchen	Qty	Description	Purchased	Cost
Knives - steak				
Knives - tomato				
Lazy Susan				
Linen Napkins/Holders				
Low ball glasses				
Marble cheese pad				
Measuring cups				
Measuring spoons				
Meat fork				
Meat tenderizers				
Milk and juice glass				
Mixing bowls				
Muffin tins (large muffins, small muffins)				
Napkin holder				
Napkin rings				
Napkins				
Non-perishables				
Olive Knives				
Omelet pan				
Open or covered vegetable dishes				
Oven mitts				
Paper bags				
Paper Napkins/Towels				
Paper party plates				
Paper towel dispenser				
Pasta strainer				
Pasta/stockpot insert				
Pastry board				
Pepper grinder				
Pie pans				
Pitchers - crystal, ceramic, glass				
Pizza pans				
Pizza stone				
Placemat sets				
Plants, planters				
Plastic ware				
Plates - bread				
Plates - dessert				
Plates - dinner				
Plates - salad				
Popover pans				
Potholders				
Pots, Pans, Lids				
Punch bowl set				

Kitchen	Qty	Description	Purchased	Cost
Quiche pan				
Recycling Can				
Refrigerated/frozen				
Refrigerator magnets				
Relish trays				
Rice cooker				
Roasters				
Rolling pin				
Rotisserie				
Rugs				
Salad bowl				
Salad spinner				
Salad tongs				
Salt/Pepper shakers				
Sandwich/plastic Bags				
Saucepots				
Saucers				
Sauté pans				
Sconce				
Sea salt grinder				
Serving spoons				
Serving trays				
Shades, blinds, curtains				
Sharpening block				
Shelving/Brackets				
Shot glasses				
Silverware holder				
Skillets				
Small Kitchen Utensils				
Smoke Detector/Batteries				
Soufflé pan				
Spatulas				
Spice Rake				
Spices				
Sponges				
Spring form pans				
Square cake pans				
Stockpots				
Sugar and creamer set				
Tea kettle				
Telephone				
Thermometer				
Thermos/Lunchboxes				
Timer				

Kitchen	Qty	Description	Purchased	Cost
Trash Can/Bags				
Trash Compactor				
Trivets				
Turkey baster				
TV tray set				
Vegetable steamer				
Warming tray				
Wastebasket				
Window Treatments				
Wine glasses				
Wine opener				
Wire cooling racks				
Wire splatter screen				
Wire whisks				
Wok				
Wooden spoons				

Notes:

Laundry Room	Qty	Description	Purchased	Cost
Clothes hamper				
Clothes hangers				
Clothes sorter				
Dryer sheets				
Fabric softener				
Ironing board				
Ironing spray				
Shelving				
Shelving/Brackets				
Stain spray				
Storage baskets				
Washer soap				

Notes:

Linens	Qty	Description	Purchased	Cost
Bath towels				
Bed ruffle				
Bedspread				
Blankets				
Cedar mothballs				
Comforters				
Cotton blankets				
Dishcloths				
Dishtowels				
Down covers				
Duvet				
Duvet covers				
Duvet/Cover				
Electric blanket				
Electric blankets				
Fitted sheets				
Flat sheets				
Hand towels				
Holiday tablecloths				
Kitchen towels				
Linen table napkins				
Mattress pad				
Pillow protectors				
Pillowcases				
Pillows/Cases				
Quilts				
Runners and tablecloths (every day)				
Sheet sets				
Sheets/Blankets				
Single sheets				
Sleeping bags/Cases				
Slipcovers				
Tablecloth				
Tablecloths/Runners				
Washcloths				
Wool blankets				

Notes:

Living room	Qty	Description	Purchased	Cost
Air conditioner (room)				
Bookends				
Books/Magazines				
bric-a-brack				
Cable organizer				
Candle holders				
Candles				
CDs				
Clock				
Collectibles				
Curtains/Rods/Brackets				
Draperies				
Drink coasters				
Fireplace screen				
Fireplace tools				
Fireplace wood holder				
Floor lamp				
Flower vases				
Magnifying glass				
Matches/Logs				
Mirrors				
Paperweights				
Rugs				
Shades, blinds, curtains				
Table lamps				
Telephone				
Vases				
Wall art, paintings, pictures				
Wastebasket				
Window hardware				

Notes:

Master bathroom	Qty	Description	Purchased	Cost
Air conditioner (room)				
Bath mat				
Bath soap and gels				
Bathtub/Jacuzzi				
Books or magazines				
Candle holders				
Candles				
Ceiling - ceiling fan				
Cleaning supplies				
Clock and/or clock radio				
Clothes hamper				
Cosmetics				
Frames				
Hair dryer, curling iron, electric rollers, toothbrush				
Heating pad				
Mirrors				
Non-prescription medicines				
Prescription medicines				
Rugs				
Scale				
Shades, blinds, curtains				
Shower curtain rings				
Shower curtain/liner				
Shower hardware (shower head, handles)				
Sink hardware (faucets, handles)				
Soap dish				
Telephone				
Tissue holder				
Toothbrush holder				
Toothbrushes				
Tweezers, razors, deodorant, perfumes				
Wastebasket				
Water glass				

Notes:

Men's accessories / clothing	Qty	Description	Purchased	Cost
Active wear				
Athletic shoes				
Athletic wear				
Blazers				
Boots				
Bracelets				
Cap				
Cuff links				
Dress pants				
Dress Shirts				
Earrings				
Gloves				
Hats				
Holiday - formal occasion				
Jackets				
Jeans				
Leather Coat				
Necklaces				
Neckties				
Outerwear				
Pants				
Polo Shirts				
Rain Coat				
Rings				
Robe				
Sandals				
Shirts (buttoned down)				
Shirts (pullover)				
Shoes				
Ski wear				
Sleepwear				
Socks				
Sports team wear				
Suits				
Suspenders				
Sweaters				
Swimwear				
Tie tacks, pins				
T-shirts				
Turtlenecks				
Undergarments				
Uniform				
Vest				

Men's accessories / clothing	Qty	Description	Purchased	Cost
Watches				
Winter Coat				
Belts/suspenders/hats/				

Office	Qty	Description	Purchased	Cost
Air Conditioner (room)				
Audio Recorder/Tapes				
Books				
Briefcase				
Calculator				
Calendars				
CD/DVD blanks				
Ceiling - ceiling fan				
Chair cushion				
Chair mat				
Clock				
Copier				
Curtains/Rods/Brackets				
Dry erase markers				
Envelopes				
Erasers				
File folders/Tabs				
Filing cabinets				
Hand hole punch				
Index cards				
Lamps				
Letter opener				
Light bulbs				
Magazines				
Magnifying glass				
Mail weight scale				
Memory sticks				
Microphones				
Mirrors				
Mousepad				
Office supplies - misc				
Paper clips/Holder				
Paper cutter				
Paper shredder				
Paper, printer ink				
Paperweights				
PDA				
Pens/Pencils/Holders				

Office	Qty	Description	Purchased	Cost
Picture albums				
Pictures/Frames				
Post it notes				
Printer/Ink cartridges				
Rubber bands				
Rug/Rug pad				
Rulers and squares				
Safe				
Scanner				
Scissors				
Shades, blinds, curtains				
Shelving/Brackets				
Spare batteries				
Spare eyeglasses				
Spare keys/Fob/Ring				
Stapler/Staples/Puller				
Stationary/Stamps				
Tape/Tape holder				
Telephone				
Three-hole punch				
White Board				

Office / Documents	Qty	Description	Purchased	Cost
Address book				
Appliance manuals				
Awards/plaques				
Birth certificates				
Business documentation				
Car titles				
Diplomas, awards, certificates				
House title				
Identification cards				
Insurance papers				
Library cards				
Loan documents				
Marriage license				
Mortgage documents				
Passports/Legal docs.				
Personal/business files				
Spare credit cards				
Warranties				

Pantry/closet	Qty	Description	Purchased	Cost
Broom				
Cleaning supplies				
Coat hangers				
Feather duster				
Mop and bucket				
Scrub brushes				
Supplies				
Vacuum				

Pets	Qty	Description	Purchased	Cost
Aquarium/Pump/Décor				
Bird cage/Food				
Collars and tags				
Fabric carrying bags				
Fish food				
Leashes				
Litterbox liners				
Litterbox/Litter/Scoop				
Pet beds and toys				
Pet crates				
Pet food bowls				
Pet food storage units				
Pet medications				
Pet trash bags				
Portable fencing				
Water containers				

Notes:

Storage	Qty	Description	Purchased	Cost
Camping supplies				
Clothes				
Crutches/Wheelchair				
Exterior décor				
Folding card table/Cots				
Games/Puzzles				
High chair/Stroller				
Holiday décor				
Luggage/Wheelies				
Magazines/Books				
Personal/Business files				
Photographs/Slides				
Photos/Albums				
Slide projector/Screen				
Sporting equipment				
Toys				
Walker/Bath support				

Notes:

Women's accessories / clothing	Qty	Description	Purchased	Cost
Active wear				
Blazers				
Boots				
Bracelets (wrist and ankle)				
Dress pants				
Earrings				
Fur coat				
Holiday dresses - formal dresses				
Jackets				
Jeans				
Leather coat				
Necklaces				
Outerwear (coats, scarves, gloves)				
Pants				
Pins				
Rings				
Sandals				
Shirts (buttoned down)				
Shirts (pullover)				
Shoes				
Skirts				
Sleepwear				
Sneakers				
Socks				
Suits				
Sweaters				
Swimsuit				
Turtlenecks				
Undergarments				
Watches				
Winter coat				
Work dresses				

Notes:

Workshop	Qty	Description	Purchased	Cost
Calendars				
Corkboard				
Curtains/Rods/Brackets				
Dremel tools/Bits				
Drill bits				
Duct/Masking tape				
Dust vacuum				
Extension cords				
Gloves/Goggles				
Glues/Clamps/Files				
Hammers/Pliers				
Hand and power tools				
Levels/Rulers				
Light bulbs				
Lumber				
Magnetic tools				
Metal brackets				
Nails/Screws				
Nuts/Bolts/Washers				
Organizer/Cans/Hooks				
Pictures/Frames				
Planers/Sandpaper				
Punches/Awls				
Roofing squares				
Rope/Chains				
Screwdrivers				
Shelving/Brackets				
Shop vacuum				
Standing fan				
Storage units				
Tool chests				

Appendix 3

Adjuster's Estimate

This is an excerpt, the entire document can be found at https://www.from-the-ash.us/worksheets/

Living Room

	Description	Quantity			Cost	RCV	Depr	ACV
53	R&R Joist - floor or ceiling - 2x8 w/blocking 16"	140.00	SF		2.55	357.00	(14.21)	342.79
54	Seal stud wall for odor control	546.67	SF		0.48	262.40	0.00	262.40
55	Seal floor or ceiling joist system	99.50	SF		0.59	58.71	0.00	58.71
56	R&R 1/2" drywall - hung, taped, floated, ready for paint (RFP)	768.67	SF		1.67	1283.68	(54.58)	1229.10
57	Seal then paint the walls and ceiling (2 coats)	768.67	SF		0.78	599.56	(149.89)	449.67
58	R&R Chair rail- 2 1/2"	68.33	LF		2.63	179.71	(16.26)	163.45
59	Paint chair rail - 2 coats	68.33	LF		0.83	56.71	(14.18)	42.53
60	R&R Bookcase - built in - 10" - (SF of face area)	21.56	SF		10.31	222.28	(21.34)	200.94
61	Seal & paint bookcase	21.56	SF		1.48	31.91	(7.98)	23.93
62	R&R Door opening (jamb & casing) - 32" to 36" wide - paint grade	1.00	EA		93.40	93.40	(8.98)	84.42
63	R&R Door opening (jamb & casing) - 36" to 60" wide - paint grade	1.00	EA		109.26	109.26	(10.56)	98.70
64	R&R Door opening (jamb & casing) - 60" or wider - paint grade	1.00	EA		128.05	128.05	(12.44)	115.61
65	Paint door/window opening - 2 coats (p/s)	6.00	EA		18.03	108.18	(27.05)	81.13
66	Paint door/window opening - large - 2 coats (p/s)	4.00	EA		21.20	84.80	(21.20)	63.60
67	&R Interior door unit	1.00	EA		166.35	166.35	(15.55)	150.80
68	R&R Exterior door - solid core lauan/mahogany or birch flush	1.00	EA		222.33	222.33	(21.00)	201.33
69	Paint door slab only - 2 coats (p/s)	4.00	EA		17.85	71.40	(17.85)	53.55
70	R&R Door knob - interior	2.00	EA		43.23	86.46	(14.40)	72.06
71	R&R Baseboard - 3 1/4"	68.33	LF		2.83	193.37	(17.49)	175.88
72	Paint baseboard - two coats	68.33	LF		0.83	56.71	(14.18)	42.53
73	R&R Base shoe	68.33	LF		1.14	77.89	(7.11)	70.78
74	Seal & paint base shoe or quarter round	68.33	LF		0.46	31.43	(7.86)	23.57
75	Sand, stain, and finish wood floor	222.00	SF		3.42	759.24	(151.85)	607.39
76	Additional coats of finish (per coat)	222.00	SF		0.78	173.16	(34.63)	138.53
77	Add for dustless floor sanding	222.00	SF		1.00	222.00	(44.40)	177.60
78	R&R Ceiling fan & light	1.00	EA		230.49	230.49	(54.90)	175.59
79	R&R Outlet	3.00	EA		15.20	45.60	(9.23)	36.37
80	R&R Switch	1.00	EA		15.20	15.20	(3.08)	12.12
81	R&R Dimmer switch	1.00	EA		35.45	35.45	(8.14)	27.31
82	R&R Phone, TV, or speaker outlet	2.00	EA		18.91	37.82	(8.10)	29.72
	Total - Living Room					6000.55	(788.44)	5212.11

Entry

	Description	Quantity		Cost	RCV	Depr	ACV
83	Seal stud wall for odor control	342.00	SF	0.48	164.16	0.00	164.16
84	Seal floor or ceiling joist system	58.24	SF	0.59	34.36	0.00	34.36
85	R&R Batt insulation - 4" - R13	21.00	SF	0.79	16.59	(0.61)	15.98
86	R&R 1/2" drywall- hung, taped, floated, RTP	400.24	SF	1.67	668.40	(28.42)	639.98
87	Seal then paint the walls and ceiling (2 coats)	400.24	SF	0.78	312.19	(78.05)	234.14
88	R&R Baseboard - 3 1/4"	42.75	LF	2.83	120.98	(10.94)	110.04
89	Paint baseboard - one coat	42.75	LF	0.54	23.09	(5.77)	17.32
90	R&R Base shoe	42.75	LF	1.14	48.74	(4.45)	44.29
91	Seal & paint base shoe or quarter round	42.75	LF	0.46	19.67	(4.92)	14.75
92	R&R Exterior door - insulated - High grade	1.00	EA	447.50	447.50	(43.52)	403.98
93	R&R Glass light, up to 24" x 24"	1.00	EA	137.77	137.77	(12.70)	125.07
94	R&R Door lockset & dead bolt - High grade	1.00	EA	112.23	112.23	(10.36)	101.87
95	R&R Storm door assembly - High grade	1.00	EA	244.45	244.45	(23.43)	221.02
96	R&R Interior door unit	1.00	EA	166.35	166.35	(15.55)	150.80
97	R&R Door knob - interior	1.00	EA	43.23	43.23	(3.60)	39.63
98	Paint door slab only - 2 coats (p/s)	4.00	EA	17.85	71.40	(17.85)	53.55
99	Paint door/window opening - 2 coats (p/s)	3.00	EA	18.03	54.09	(13.52)	40.57
100	R&R Closet shelf and rod package	5.17	LF	23.21	119.99	(10.51)	109.48
101	Paint - closet package (shelf, jamb & casing)	1.00	EA	30.45	30.45	(7.61)	22.84
102	R&R Light fixture	1.00	EA	56.39	56.39	(12.90)	43.49
103	R&R Smoke detector	1.00	EA	42.21	42.21	(8.95)	33.26
104	R&R Switch	3.00	EA	15.20	45.60	(3.69)	41.91
105	Clean floor, strip & wax	58.24	SF	0.53	30.87	0.00	30.87
	Total - Entry				**3010.71**	**(317.35)**	**2693.36**

Kitchen

	Description	Quantity		Cost	RCV	Depr	ACV
238	Seal stud wall for odor control	558.68	SF	0.48	268.17	0.00	268.17
239	Seal floor or ceiling joist system	267.28	SF	0.59	157.70	0.00	157.70
240	R&R Batt insulation - 4" - R13	279.34	SF	0.79	220.68	(8.10)	212.58
241	R&R 1/2" drywall HTFRFP	267.28	SF	1.67	446.36	(18.98)	427.38
242	Seal then paint the ceiling	267.28	SF	0.78	208.48	(52.12)	156.36
243	R&R Paneling	558.68	SF	1.99	1111.77	(202.24)	909.53
244	Seal & paint paneling	558.68	SF	0.68	379.90	(94.98)	284.92
245	R&R Cove molding - 3/4"	69.83	LF	1.08	75.41	(6.84)	68.57
246	Paint cove molding - one coat	69.83	LF	0.37	25.84	(6.46)	19.38
247	R&R Wallpaper - High grade	225.00	SF	2.37	533.25	(105.75)	427.50
248	R&R Door opening (jamb & casing)	1.00	EA	93.40	93.40	(8.98)	84.42
249	R&R Window stool & apron	9.00	LF	5.65	50.85	(4.69)	46.16
250	R&R Casing - 2 1/4"	35.00	LF	1.81	63.35	(5.32)	58.03
251	Seal & paint wood window (p/s)	3.00	EA	25.40	76.20	(19.05)	57.15
252	Paint door/window opening - 2 coats (p/s)	5.00	EA	18.03	90.15	(22.54)	67.61
253	Clean window unit (p/s) 20 SF	3.00	EA	8.45	25.35	0.00	25.35
254	R&R Motorized shades	1.00	SF	32.05	32.05	0.00	32.05

	Description	Quantity		Cost	RCV	Depr	ACV
255	R&R Shutters - wood - louvered	2.00	EA	245.97	491.94	(48.47)	443.47
256	Seal & paint window shutters p/s	4.00	EA	19.19	76.76	(19.19)	57.57
257	R&R Window drapery - hardware	2.00	EA	80.39	160.78	(31.00)	129.78
258	R&R Cabinetry upper (wall) units	14.50	LF	103.95	1507.28	(361.12)	1146.16
259	R&R Cabinet valance	5.11	LF	44.50	227.40	(55.27)	172.13
260	R&R Cabinetry - lower (base) units	11.85	LF	166.56	1973.74	(480.61)	1493.13
261	R&R Cabinet panels - side, end, or back	12.00	SF	14.92	179.04	(41.40)	137.64
262	R&R Countertop - Flat laid plastic laminate	14.17	LF	37.35	529.25	(123.49)	405.76
263	R&R Wood appliance panel- average grade	0.00	SF	31.16	0.00	0.00	0.00
264	Add-on for mitered comer Countertop)	1.00	EA	59.13	59.13	(14.78)	44.35
265	R&R 4" backsplash for countertop	14.17	LF	7.47	105.85	(24.62)	81.23
266	R&R Cabinet knob average grade	21.00	EA	6.76	141.96	(31.97)	109.99
267	R&R Sink - double	1.00	EA	306.61	306.61	(73.77)	232.84
268	R&R Sink faucet	1.00	EA	147.26	147.26	(34.11)	113.15
269	R&R Garbage disposer	1.00	EA	174.45	174.45	(32.00)	142.45
270	R&R Dishwasher	1.00	EA	397.52	397.52	(76.41)	321.11
271	R&R Range hood	1.00	EA	166.48	166.48	(31.84)	134.64
272	Detach & Reset Range -freestanding electric	1.00	EA	47.93	47.93	0.00	47.93
273	R&R Baseboard - 3 1/4"	69.83	LF	2.83	197.61	(17.88)	179.73
274	R&R Base shoe	69.83	LF	1.14	79.60	(7.26)	72.34
275	Paint baseboard - one coat	69.83	LF	0.54	37.71	(9.43)	28.28
276	Seal & paint base shoe or quarter round	69.83	LF	0.46	32.12	(8.03)	24.09
277	R&R Underlayment - 1 1/4 mahogany plywood "	120.00	SF	2.19	262.80	(28.80)	234.00
278	Remove Vinyl floor covering (sheet goods)	120.00	SF	0.54	64.80	0.00	64.80
279	Vinyl floor covering (sheet goods) 15 % waste added	138.00	SF	3.31	456.78	(91.36)	365.42
280	R&R Carpet pad	165.00	SF	0.88	145.20	(33.41)	111.79
281	Remove Carpet	165.00	SF	0.15	24.75	0.00	24.75
282	Carpet 15% waste added	189.75	SF	3.12	592.02	(148.01)	444.01
283	R&R Ceiling fan & light	1.00	EA	230.49	230.49	(54.90)	175.59
284	R&R Recessed light fixture	1.00	EA	95.06	95.06	(22.16)	72.90
285	R&R Fluorescent light fixture	1.00	EA	86.29	86.29	(19.56)	66.73
286	R&R Cold air return cover	1.00	EA	27.71	27.71	(1.20)	26.51
287	R&R Heat/ AC register	2.00	EA	20.46	40.92	(3.93)	36.99
288	R&R Outlet	6.00	EA	15.20	91.20	(3.69)	87.51
289	R&R Switch	5.00	EA	15.20	76.00	(3.08)	72.92
290	R&R Ground fault interrupter (GFI) outlet	1.00	EA	29.18	29.18	(1.33)	27.85
291	R&R 220-volt outlet	1.00	EA	25.31	25.31	(1.12)	24.19
	Total - Kitchen				13147.84	(2491.25)	10656.59

Sunroom

	Description	Quantity		Cost	RCV	Depr	ACV
354	Seal stud wall for odor control	477.33	SF	0.48	229.12	0.00	229.12
355	Seal floor or ceiling joist system	222.33	SF	0.59	131.17	0.00	131.17
356	R&R Batt insulation - 4" - R13	358.00	SF	0.79	282.82	(10.38)	272.44
357	R&R 1/2" drywall - hung, taped, floated, RFP	699.67	SF	1.67	1168.45	(49.68)	1118.77
358	R&R Wallpaper - High grade	477.33	SF	2.37	1131.27	(224.35)	906.92
359	R&R Wallpaper border - High grade	59.67	LF	2.69	160.51	(34.01)	126.50
360	R&R Casing - 2 1/4"	160.00	LF	1.81	289.60	(24.32)	265.28
361	Paint door/window trim & jamb - 2 coats p/s	8.00	EA	18.03	144.24	(36.06)	108.18
362	Paint door/window trim & jamb - Large - 2 coats (p/s)	1.00	EA	21.20	21.20	(5.30)	15.90
363	R&R Baseboard - 3 1/4"	59.67	LF	2.83	168.87	(15.28)	153.59
364	Paint baseboard - one coat	59.67	LF	0.54	32.22	(8.06)	24.16
365	R&R Ceiling fan & light - High grade	1.00	EA	360.46	360.46	(87.39)	273.07
366	R&R Window blind - horizontal or vertical	8.00	EA	90.78	726.24	(169.94)	556.30
367	R&R Window blind - horizontal or vertical - Extra large	1.00	EA	169.42	169.42	(40.90)	128.52
368	R&R Baseboard electric heater - 8' - hydronic	1.00	EA	380.73	380.73	(93.02)	287.71
369	R&R Outlet	5.00	EA	15.20	76.00	(6.15)	69.85
370	R&R Switch	1.00	EA	15.20	15.20	(2.46)	12.74
371	R&R Carpet pad	222.33	SF	0.88	195.65	(54.03)	141.62
372	Remove Carpet	222.33	SF	0.15	33.35	0.00	33.35
373	Carpet -15 % waste added	255.68	SF	3.12	797.72	(239.32)	558.40
	Total - Sunroom				**6514.24**	**(1100.65)**	**5413.59**

Appendix 4

Contractor's Estimate

This is an excerpt, the entire document can be found at https://www.from-the-ash.us/worksheets/

Sitting Room

	DESCRIPTION	Burden	Labor	Material	Eqpt	Market	TOTAL
35 a	Remove Joist - floor or ceiling - 2x6 – w/blocking - 16" oc	14.00	39.20	0.00	0.00	0.00	53.20
35 b	Joist - floor or ceiling - 2x6 - w/blocking - 16" oc	26.60	91.00	96.60	0.00	0.00	214.20
36	2" x 4" X 18' #2 & better Fir / Larch (material only)	0.00	0.00	5.47	0.00	2.17	7.64
37	2" x 6" X 18' #2 & better Fir / Larch (material only)	0.00	0.00	8.76	0.00	3.24	12.00
38 a	Remove 1/2" Drywall- hung, taped, with smooth wall finish	49.01	126.01	0.00	0.00	0.00	175.02
38 b	1/2" Drywall- hung, taped, with smooth wall finish	189.02	882.08	252.01	0.00	0.00	1323.11
39	Seal stud wall for odor control	43.25	144.17	43.25	0.00	0.00	230.67
40	Seal floor or ceiling joist system	11.94	37.81	8.96	0.00	0.00	58.71
41 a	Remove Ceiling fan & light	2.93	7.96	0.00	0.00	0.00	10.89
41 b	Ceiling fan & light	20.15	114.45	0.00	84.62	0.38	219.60
42 a	Remove Chair rail- 2 1/2"	4.10	10.55	0.00	0.00	0.00	14.65
42 b	Chair rail - 2 1/2"	12.89	51.55	74.98	0.00	0.00	139.42
43	Paint chair rail- two coats	10.54	33.39	4.69	0.00	0.00	48.62
44	Seal then paint the walls and ceiling (2 coats) - 2 colors	84.01	273.03	84.01	0.00	147.00	588.05
45 a	Remove Cold air return cover	1.96	5.32	0.00	0.00	0.00	7.28
45 b	Cold air return cover	2.90	18.08	27.14	0.00	0.02	48.14
46 a	Remove Heat AC register	0.44	1.18	0.00	0.00	0.00	1.62
46 b	Heat AC register	2.40	14.94	21.96	0.00	0.00	39.30
47 a	Remove Bookcase - built in - 10" - (SF off ace area)	2.37	6.47	0.00	0.00	0.00	8.84
47 b	Bookcase - built in - 10" - (SF offace area)	19.19	78.05	116.20	0.00	0.00	213.44
48	Seal & paint bookcase	5.94	18.92	7.70	0.00	0.00	32.56
49 a	Remove Trim board - 1" x 4" - installed (pine)	1.20	3.40	0.00	0.00	0.00	4.60
49 b	Trim board - 1" x 4" - installed (pine)	5.00	20.40	25.60	0.00	1.20	52.20
50	Seal & paint trim	3.60	11.40	1.60	0.00	0.00	16.60
51 a	Remove Rosette - corner block - 3/4" x 3 1/2" - Pine	0.66	1.80	0.00	0.00	0.00	2.46
51 b	Rosette - corner block - 3/4" x 3 1/2" - Pine	1.68	6.86	5.34	0.00	0.00	13.88
52 a	Remove Door opening (jamb & casing) - 32" to 36"wide - paint grade	0.98	2.66	0.00	0.00	0.00	3.64
52 b	Door opening (jamb & casing) - 32" to 36"wide - paint grade	6.53	26.51	55.50	0.00	1.22	89.76
53 a	Remove Door opening (jamb & casing) - 36" to 60"wide - paint grade	0.98	2.66	0.00	0.00	0.00	3.64
53 b	Door opening (jamb & casing) - 36" to 60"wide - paint grade	7.83	31.79	66.00	0.00	0.00	105.62
54a	Remove Door opening (jamb & casing) - 60" or wider - paint grade	0.98	2.66	0.00	0.00	0.00	3.64

	DESCRIPTION	Burden	Labor	Material	Eqpt	Market	TOTAL
54 b	Door opening (jamb & casing) - 60" or wider - paint grade	8.90	36.14	79.37	0.00	0.00	124.41
55 a	Remove Interior door unit	2.91	7.91	0.00	0.00	0.00	10.82
55 b	Interior door unit	7.51	30.49	107.62	9.91	0.00	155.53
56 a	Remove Exterior door - solid core lauan I mahogany or birch flush	3.32	9.03	0.00	0.00	0.00	12.35
56 b	Exterior door - solid core lauan 1 mahogany or birch flush	11.26	45.74	152.98	0.00	0.00	209.98
57	Paint door or window opening - 2 coats (per side)	21.48	69.66	17.04	0.00	0.00	108.18
58	Paint door or window opening - Large - 2 coats (per side)	16.84	54.64	13.32	0.00	0.00	84.80
59	Doorknob - interior	5.58	24.90	41.54	0.00	0.00	72.02
60 a	Remove Baseboard - 3 1/4"	4.11	11.71	0.00	0.00	0.00	15.82
60 b	Baseboard - 3 1/4"	14.65	59.75	75.56	0.00	0.00	149.96
61	Paint baseboard - two coats	10.54	33.39	4.69	0.00	0.00	48.62
62 a	Remove Base shoe	1.76	4.10	0.00	0.00	0.00	5.86
62b	Base shoe	6.44	26.36	28.12	0.00	0.00	60.92
63	Seal & paint base shoe or quarter round	5.27	17.58	4.10	0.00	0.00	26.95
65	Sand, stain, and finish wood floor	87.80	425.83	160.23	76.83	0.00	750.69
66	Additional coats of finish (per coat)	19.76	92.19	28.53	30.73	0.00	171.21
67	Add for dustless floor sanding	0.00	0.00	219.50	0.00	0.00	219.50
68 a	Remove Outlet	2.34	6.36	0.00	0.00	0.00	8.70
68 b	Outlet	4.05	23.10	9.75	0.00	0.00	36.90
69 a	Remove Switch	0.78	2.12	0.00	0.00	0.00	2.90
69 b	Switch	1.35	7.70	3.25	0.00	0.00	12.30
70 a	Remove Dimmer switch	0.78	2.12	0.00	0.00	0.00	2.90
70 b	Dimmer switch	1.35	7.70	23.50	0.00	0.00	32.55
71 a	Remove Phone, TV, or speaker outlet	1.46	3.96	0.00	0.00	0.00	5.42
71 b	Phone, TV, or speaker outlet	15.40	2.70	14.30	0.00	0.00	32.40
72 a	Remove 1/2" drywall- hung, taped, with smooth wall finish	39.79	15.48	0.00	0.00	0.00	55.27
72 b	1/2" Drywall - hung, taped, with smooth wall finish	278.54	59.69	79.57	0.00	0.00	417.80
73 a	Remove 1/2" Drywall- hung, taped, floated, ready for paint	78.58	30.56	0.00	0.00	0.00	109.14
73 b	1/2" drywall- hung, taped, floated, ready for paint	353.61	78.58	179.00	8.73	0.00	619.92
74	Seal stud wall for odor control	130.97	39.29	39.29	0.00	0.00	209.55
75	Seal floor or ceiling joist system	84.01	26.53	19.89	0.00	0.00	130.43
76 a	Remove Batt insulation - 4" - R13	49.12	19.64	0.00	0.00	0.00	68.76
76 b	Batt insulation - 4" - R13	72.03	13.10	104.77	0.00	0.00	189.90
77 a	Remove Ceiling fan & light - High grade	7.96	2.93	0.00	0.00	0.00	10.89
77 b	Ceiling fan & light - High grade	114.45	20.15	198.40	0.00	16.57	349.57
78	Wallpaper (per roll)	292.68	94.14	372.24	0.00	0.00	759.06
79	Wallpaper border - High grade	36.30	11.90	87.46	0.00	0.00	135.66
80	Prep wall for wallpaper	117.87	39.29	0.00	0.00	0.00	157.16
81 a	Remove Casing - 2 1/4"	33.60	12.80	0.00	0.00	0.00	46.40

	DESCRIPTION	Burden	Labor	Material	Eqpt	Market	TOTAL
81 b	Casing - 2 1/4"	86.40	20.80	136.00	0.00	0.00	243.20
82	Paint door/window trim & jamb - 2 coats (per side)	92.88	28.64	22.72	0.00	0.00	144.24
83	Paint door/window trim & jamb - Large - 2 coats (per side)	13.66	4.21	3.33	0.00	0.00	21.20
84 a	Remove Window blind - horizontal or vertical	34.00	12.48	0.00	0.00	0.00	46.48
84 b	Window blind - horizontal or vertical	209.68	47.04	408.00	0.00	15.04	679.76
85 a	Remove Window blind - horizontal or vertical - Extra large	4.25	1.56	0.00	0.00	0.00	5.81
85 b	Window blind - horizontal or vertical - Extra large	35.46	7.95	120.20	0.00	0.00	163.61
86 a	Remove Baseboard - 3 114"	10.71	3.76	0.00	0.00	0.00	14.47
86 b	Baseboard - 3 114"	54.65	13.40	69.11	0.00	0.00	137.16
87	Paint baseboard - two coats	30.54	9.64	4.29	0.00	0.00	44.47
88 a	Remove Baseboard electric heater - 8' - hydronic	6.33	2.33	0.00	0.00	0.00	8.66
88 b	Baseboard electric heater - 8' - hydronic	65.40	11.51	295.16	0.00	0.00	372.07
89 a	Remove Outlet	10.60	3.90	0.00	0.00	0.00	14.50
89 b	Outlet	38.50	6.75	16.25	0.00	0.00	61.50
90 a	Remove Switch	2.12	0.78	0.00	0.00	0.00	2.90
90 b	Switch	7.70	1.35	3.25	0.00	0.00	12.30
91 a	Remove Carpet pad	11.05	4.42	0.00	0.00	0.00	15.47
91 b	Carpet pad	15.47	2.21	137.06	0.00	24.32	179.06
92	Remove Carpet	24.31	8.85	0.00	0.00	0.00	33.16
93	Carpet	107.55	21.51	602.28	14.34	0.00	745.68
	Sitting Room						12309.90

Kitchen

	DESCRIPTION	Burden	Labor	Material	Eqpt	Market	TOTAL
94 a	Remove 1/2" drywall- hung, taped, with smooth wall finish	48.11	18.71	0.00	0.00	0.00	66.82
94 b	1/2" Drywall- hung, taped, with smooth wall finish	336.77	72.17	96.22	0.00	0.00	505.16
95	Seal then paint the ceiling (2 coats)	90.87	26.73	32.07	0.00	58.81	208.48
96 a	Remove Paneling	67.35	25.91	0.00	0.00	0.00	93.26
96 b	Paneling	492.21	124.35	321.22	0.00	0.00	937.78
97	Seal & paint paneling	133.67	40.41	37.31	0.00	0.00	211.39
98 a	Remove Cove molding - 3/4"	4.89	2.09	0.00	0.00	0.00	6.98
98 b	Cove molding - 3/4"	31.42	7.68	29.33	0.00	0.00	68.43
99	Paint cove molding - two coats	26.54	8.38	4.18	0.00	0.00	39.10
100	Wallpaper(per roll)	146.34	47.07	186.12	0.00	0.00	379.53
101	Prep wall for wallpaper	60.75	20.25	0.00	0.00	0.00	81.00
102	Seal stud wall for odor control	155.43	46.63	46.63	0.00	0.00	248.69
103	Seal floor or ceiling joist system	55.96	17.67	13.27	0.00	0.00	86.90
104 a	Remove Ceiling fan & light	7.96	2.93	0.00	0.00	0.00	10.89
104 b	Ceiling fan & light	114.45	20.15	84.62	0.00	0.38	219.60
105 a	Remove Recessed light fixture	4.70	1.73	0.00	0.00	0.00	6.43
105 b	Recessed light fixture	50.24	8.84	29.55	0.00	0.00	88.63

	DESCRIPTION	Burden	Labor	Material	Eqpt	Market	TOTAL
106a	Remove Fluorescent - one tube - 2' - fixture w/lens	5.88	2.16	0.00	0.00	0.00	8.04
106 b	Fluorescent - one tube - 2' - fixture w/lens	28.64	5.04	23.88	0.00	0.00	57.56
107 a	Remove Batt insulation - 4" - R13	38.86	15.54	0.00	0.00	0.00	54.40
107 b	Batt insulation - 4" - R13	57.00	10.36	82.89	0.00	0.00	150.25
108 a	Remove Door opening (jamb & casing) - 32" to 36" wide - paint grade	2.66	0.98	0.00	0.00	0.00	3.64
108 b	Door opening (jamb & casing) - 32" to 36" wide - paint grade	26.51	6.53	55.50	0.00	1.22	89.76
109 a	Remove Window stool & apron	2.88	1.08	0.00	0.00	0.00	3.96
109 b	Window stool & apron	19.26	4.77	22.86	0.00	0.00	46.89
110 a	Remove Casing - 2 1/4"	7.35	2.80	0.00	0.00	0.00	10.15
110 b	Casing - 2 1/4"	18.90	4.55	29.75	0.00	0.00	53.20
111	Clean window unit (per side) 10 - 20 SF	19.38	5.91	0.06	0.00	0.00	25.35
112	Seal & paint wood window (per side)	48.63	15.00	12.57	0.00	0.00	76.20
113	Paint door or window opening - 2 coats (per side)	58.05	17.90	14.20	0.00	0.00	90.15
114 a	Remove Shutters - wood - louvered	5.26	1.94	0.00	0.00	0.00	7.20
114 b	Shutters - wood - louvered	68.58	16.16	400.00	0.00	0.00	484.74
115 a	Remove Window blind - horizontal or vertical	4.25	1.56	0.00	0.00	0.00	5.81
115 b	Window blind - horizontal or vertical	26.21	5.88	51.00	0.00	1.88	84.97
116 a	Remove Window drapery - hardware	4.24	1.56	0.00	0.00	0.00	5.80
116b	Window drapery - hardware	52.42	11.76	90.80	0.00	0.00	154.98
117 a	Remove Cabinetry - upper (wall) units	46.00	16.83	0.00	0.00	0.00	62.83
117 b	Cabinetry - upper (wall) units	298.76	73.57	1073.16	0.00	0.00	1445.49
118 a	Remove Cabinet valance	4.65	1.69	0.00	0.00	0.00	6.34
118 b	Cabinet valance	13.39	3.27	204.40	0.00	0.00	221.06
119 a	Remove Cabinetry - lower (base) units	37.53	13.74	0.00	0.00	0.00	51.27
119 b	Cabinetry - lower (base) units	243.79	60.03	1616.98	0.00	0.00	1920.80
120 a	Remove Cabinet panels - side, end, or back	9.84	3.60	0.00	0.00	0.00	13.44
120 b	Cabinet panels - side, end, or back	58.92	14.52	92.16	0.00	0.00	165.60
121a	Remove Countertop - Flat laid plastic laminate	25.79	9.49	0.00	0.00	0.00	35.28
121 b	Countertop - Flat laid plastic laminate	100.61	24.80	368.56	0.00	0.00	493.97
122	Add-on for mitered corner (Countertop)	47.45	11.68	0.00	0.00	0.00	59.13
123 a	Remove 4" backsplash for flat laid countertop	5.39	1.98	0.00	0.00	0.00	7.37
123 b	4" backsplash for flat laid countertop	22.68	5.53	70.27	0.00	0.00	98.48
124	Cabinet knob or pull- Average grade	55.02	13.44	59.43	0.00	0.00	127.89
125 a	Remove Sink - double	8.44	3.10	0.00	0.00	0.00	11.54
125 b	Sink - double	64.92	10.42	208.54	0.00	11.19	295.07
126 a	Remove Sink faucet - Kitchen	7.91	2.91	0.00	0.00	0.00	10.82
126 b	Sink faucet - Kitchen	43.46	6.98	85.99	0.01	0.00	136.44
127 a	Remove Garbage disposer	10.55	3.88	0.00	0.00	0.00	14.43
127 b	Garbage disposer	62.45	10.03	87.54	0.00	0.00	160.02
128 a	Remove Dishwasher	11.30	4.15	0.00	0.00	0.00	15.45
128 b	Dishwasher	72.44	11.63	298.00	0.00	0.00	382.07
129a	Remove Range - freestanding - electric - High grade	8.50	3.12	0.00	0.00	0.00	11.62

	DESCRIPTION	Burden	Labor	Material	Eqpt	Market	TOTAL
129b	Range - freestanding - electric - High grade	43.95	7.74	865.73	0.00	15.16	932.58
130 a	Remove Cold air return cover	2.66	0.98	0.00	0.00	0.00	3.64
130 b	Cold air return cover	9.04	1.45	13.57	0.00	0.01	24.07
131 b	Remove Heat/AC register	1.18	0.44	0.00	0.00	0.00	1.62
131 b	Heat/AC register	14.94	2.40	21.96	0.00	0.00	39.30
132 a	Remove Baseboard - 3 1/4"	12.76	4.45	0.00	0.00	0.00	17.21
132 b	Baseboard - 3 1/4"	65.02	15.94	82.24	0.00	0.00	163.20
133	Paint baseboard - two coats	36.34	11.48	5.09	0.00	0.00	52.91
134 a	Remove Base shoe	4.47	1.91	0.00	0.00	0.00	6.38
134 b	Base shoe	28.69	7.01	30.60	0.00	0.00	66.30
135	Seal & paint base shoe or quarter round	19.13	5.74	4.46	0.00	0.00	29.33
136 a	Remove Switch	10.60	3.90	0.00	0.00	0.00	14.50
136 b	Switch	38.50	6.75	16.25	0.00	0.00	61.50
137 a	Remove Outlet	12.72	4.68	0.00	0.00	0.00	17.40
137 b	Outlet	46.20	8.10	19.50	0.00	0.00	73.80
138 a	Remove Ground fault interrupter (GFI) outlet	1.90	0.70	0.00	0.00	0.00	2.60
138 b	Ground fault interrupter (GFI) outlet	8.54	1.50	13.45	0.00	3.09	26.58
139 a	Remove 220 volt outlet	2.12	0.78	0.00	0.00	0.00	2.90
139 b	220 volt outlet	12.82	2.26	7.33	0.00	0.00	22.41
140 a	Remove Phone, TV, or speaker outlet	3.96	1.46	0.00	0.00	0.00	5.42
140 b	Phone, TV, or speaker outlet	15.40	2.70	14.30	0.00	0.00	32.40
141 a	Remove Underlayment - 1/2" particle board	99.60	19.20	0.00	0.00	0.00	118.80
141 b	Underlayment - 1/2" particle board	79.20	15.60	62.40	0.00	0.00	157.20
142	Vinyl floor covering (sheet goods)	152.64	28.80	295.20	0.00	0.00	476.64
143 a	Remove Carpet pad	8.25	3.30	0.00	0.00	0.00	11.55
143 b	Carpet pad	11.55	1.65	102.30	0.00	18.15	133.65
144 a	Remove Carpet	18.15	6.60	0.00	0.00	0.00	24.75
144 b	Carpet	74.25	14.85	415.80	9.90	0.00	514.80
145	Additional labor cost for Berber or patterned carpets	23.10	4.95	0.00	0.00	0.00	28.05
146 a	Remove Vinyl- metal transition strip	4.48	1.68	0.00	0.00	0.00	6.16
146 b	Vinyl- metal transition strip	11.90	2.24	29.54	0.00	0.00	43.68
	Kitchen/Hearth Total						13529.86

Entry

	DESCRIPTION	Burden	Labor	Material	Eqpt	Market	TOTAL
147 a	Remove 1/2" dlywall- hung, taped, with smooth wall finish	68.34	26.58	0.00	0.00	0.00	94.92
147 b	1/2" Drywall- hung, taped, with smooth wall finish	478.40	102.51	136.69	0.00	0.00	717.60
148	Seal then paint the walls and ceiling (2 coats)	129.09	37.97	45.56	0.00	83.53	296.15
149 a	Remove Light fixture	3.52	1.29	0.00	0.00	0.00	4.81
149 b	Light fixture	21.02	3.70	24.33	0.00	2.53	51.58
150	Smoke detector	18.96	3.34	13.51	0.00	0.00	35.81
151 a	Remove Exterior door - metal - insulated / wood - High grade	9.03	3.32	0.00	0.00	0.00	12.35
151 b	Exterior door - metal - insulated / wood - High	45.74	11.26	378.15	0.00	0.00	435.15

	DESCRIPTION	Burden	Labor	Material	Eqpt	Market	TOTAL
	grade						
152	Glass light, up to 24" x 24"	68.60	16.89	41.46	0.00	0.00	126.95
153	Door lockset & deadbolt - exterior	16.61	3.72	45.52	0.00	5.54	71.39
154 a	Remove Storm door assembly - High grade	7.44	2.74	0.00	0.00	0.00	10.18
154 b	Storm door assembly - High grade	51.47	12.67	170.13	0.00	0.00	234.27
155 a	Remove Interior door unit	7.91	2.91	0.00	0.00	0.00	10.82
155 b	Interior door unit	30.49	7.51	107.62	0.00	9.91	155.53
156 a	Remove Door knob - interior	5.28	1.94	0.00	0.00	0.00	7.22
156 b	Doorknob - interior	12.45	2.79	20.77	0.00	0.00	36.01
157	Paint door slab only - 2 coats (per side)	40.24	12.40	18.72	0.00	0.04	71.40
158	Paint door or window opening - 2 coats (per side)	34.83	10.74	8.52	0.00	0.00	54.09
159 a	Remove Closet shelf and rod package	10.91	4.03	0.00	0.00	0.00	14.94
159 b	Closet shelf and rod package	66.49	16.39	22.17	0.00	0.00	105.05
160	Paint - closet package (shelf, jamb & casing)	20.03	6.18	4.24	0.00	0.00	30.45
161	Seal stud wall for odor control	96.44	28.93	28.93	0.00	0.00	154.30
162	Seal floor or ceiling joist system	22.13	6.99	5.24	0.00	0.00	34.36
163 a	Remove Batt insulation	3.15	1.26	0.00	0.00	0.00	4.41
163 b	Batt Insulation - 4" - R13	4.62	0.84	6.72	0.00	0.00	12.18
164 a	Remove Baseboard - 3 1/4"	7.93	2.78	0.00	0.00	0.00	10.71
164 b	Baseboard - 3 1/4"	40.46	9.92	51.18	0.00	0.00	101.56
165	Paint baseboard - two coats	22.61	7.14	3.18	0.00	0.00	32.93
166 a	Remove Base shoe	2.77	1.20	0.00	0.00	0.00	3.97
166 b	Base shoe	17.85	4.36	19.05	0.00	0.00	41.26
167	Seal & paint base shoe or quarter round	11.90	3.57	2.78	0.00	0.00	18.25
168 a	Remove Switch	6.36	2.34	0.00	0.00	0.00	8.70
168 b	Switch	23.10	4.05	9.75	0.00	0.00	36.90
169	Clean floor, strip & wax	20.38	5.82	4.67	0.00	0.00	30.87
	ENTRY Total						2254.55

Appendix 5

Adjuster / Contractor Reconciliation

This is an excerpt, the entire document can be found at https://www.from-the-ash.us/worksheets/

Adj#	Est#	Hrs	Rate	Qty	Unit Cost	Mkt Cond	Total	Burden	Labor	Matl	Eqpt	Mkt Cond	Total	Dif
53	31b	3.94	65.02	1.00	930.26	0.00	930.26	35.44	220.86	673.96	0.00	0.00	930.26	0
54	32	4.38	23.00	426.88	0.32	0.00	136.60	25.61	76.84	4.27	29.88	0.00	136.60	0
55	33a	0.40	28.84	4.00	2.90	0.00	11.60	3.12	8.48	0.00	0.00	0.00	11.60	0
56	33b	0.56	65.01	4.00	12.30	0.00	49.20	5.40	30.80	13.00	0.00	0.00	49.20	0
57	34a	0.10	28.84	1.00	2.90	0.00	2.90	0.78	2.12	0.00	0.00	0.00	2.90	0
58	34b	0.14	65.01	1.00	12.30	0.00	12.30	1.35	7.70	3.25	0.00	0.00	12.30	0
62	35a	1.88	28.84	140.00	0.38	0.00	53.20	14.00	39.20	0.00	0.00	0.00	53.20	0
63	35b	2.66	43.82	140.00	1.53	0.00	214.20	26.60	91.00	96.60	0.00	0.00	214.20	0
64	36	0.00	0.00	1.00	7.64	2.17	7.64	0.00	0.00	5.47	0.00	2.17	7.64	0
65	37	0.00	0.00	1.00	12.00	3.24	12.00	0.00	0.00	8.76	0.00	3.24	12.00	0
67	38a	5.83	28.84	700.06	0.25	0.00	175.02	49.01	126.01	0.00	0.00	0.00	175.02	0
68	38b	21.82	49.06	700.06	1.89	0.00	1323.11	189.02	882.08	252.01	0.00	0.00	1323.11	0
69	39	4.88	38.89	480.56	0.48	0.00	230.67	43.25	144.17	43.25	0.00	0.00	230.67	0
70	40	1.27	38.89	99.50	0.59	0.00	58.71	11.94	37.81	8.96	0.00	0.00	58.71	0
71	41a	0.38	28.84	1.00	10.89	0.00	10.89	2.93	7.96	0.00	0.00	0.00	10.89	0
72	41b	2.07	65.01	1.00	219.60	0.38	219.60	20.15	114.45	0.00	84.62	0.38	219.60	0
73	42a	0.49	28.84	58.58	0.25	0.00	14.65	4.10	10.55	0.00	0.00	0.00	14.65	0
74	42b	1.34	48.09	58.58	2.38	0.00	139.42	12.89	51.55	74.98	0.00	0.00	139.42	0
75	43	1.12	38.89	58.58	0.83	0.00	48.62	10.54	33.39	4.69	0.00	0.00	48.62	0
76	44	9.00	38.89	700.06	0.84	147.00	588.05	84.01	273.03	84.01	0.00	147.00	588.05	0
78	45a	0.25	28.84	2.00	3.64	0.00	7.28	1.96	5.32	0.00	0.00	0.00	7.28	0
79	45b	0.32	65.02	2.00	24.07	0.02	48.14	2.90	18.08	27.14	0.00	0.02	48.14	0
80	46a	0.06	28.84	2.00	0.81	0.00	1.62	0.44	1.18	0.00	0.00	0.00	1.62	0
81	46b	0.27	65.02	2.00	19.65	0.00	39.30	2.40	14.94	21.96	0.00	0.00	39.30	0
82	47a	0.30	28.84	21.56	0.41	0.00	8.84	2.37	6.47	0.00	0.00	0.00	8.84	0
83	47b	2.03	48.09	21.56	9.90	0.00	213.44	19.19	78.05	116.20	0.00	0.00	213.44	0
84	48	0.64	38.89	22.00	1.48	0.00	32.56	5.94	18.92	7.70	0.00	0.00	32.56	0
85	49a	0.16	28.84	20.00	0.23	0.00	4.60	1.20	3.40	0.00	0.00	0.00	4.60	0
86	49b	0.53	48.09	20.00	2.61	1.20	52.20	5.00	20.40	25.60	0.00	1.20	52.20	0
88	50	0.38	38.89	20.00	0.83	0.00	16.60	3.60	11.40	1.60	0.00	0.00	16.60	0
89	51a	0.09	28.84	2.00	1.23	0.00	2.46	0.66	1.80	0.00	0.00	0.00	2.46	0
90	51b	0.18	48.09	2.00	6.94	0.00	13.88	1.68	6.86	5.34	0.00	0.00	13.88	0
91	52a	0.13	28.84	1.00	3.64	0.00	3.64	0.98	2.66	0.00	0.00	0.00	3.64	0
92	52b	0.69	48.09	1.00	89.76	1.22	89.76	6.53	26.51	55.50	0.00	1.22	89.76	0
93	53a	0.13	28.84	1.00	3.64	0.00	3.64	0.98	2.66	0.00	0.00	0.00	3.64	0
94	53b	0.82	48.09	1.00	105.62	0.00	105.62	7.83	31.79	66.00	0.00	0.00	105.62	0
95	54a	0.13	28.84	1.00	3.64	0.00	3.64	0.98	2.66	0.00	0.00	0.00	3.64	0
96	54b	0.94	48.09	1.00	124.41	0.00	124.41	8.90	36.14	79.37	0.00	0.00	124.41	0
97	55a	0.37	28.84	1.00	10.82	0.00	10.82	2.91	7.91	0.00	0.00	0.00	10.82	0
98	55b	0.79	48.09	1.00	155.53	0.00	155.53	7.51	30.49	107.62	9.91	0.00	155.53	0
107	56a	0.43	28.84	1.00	12.35	0.00	12.35	3.32	9.03	0.00	0.00	0.00	12.35	0

Adj#	Est#	Hrs	Rate	Qty	Unit Cost	Mkt Cond	Total	Burden	Labor	Matl	Eqpt	Mkt Cond	Total	Dif
108	56b	1.19	48.09	1.00	209.98	0.00	209.98	11.26	45.74	152.98	0.00	0.00	209.98	0
110	57	2.34	38.89	6.00	18.03	0.00	108.18	21.48	69.66	17.04	0.00	0.00	108.18	0
111	58	1.84	38.89	4.00	21.20	0.00	84.80	16.84	54.64	13.32	0.00	0.00	84.80	0
112	59	0.70	43.83	2.00	36.01	0.00	72.02	5.58	24.90	41.54	0.00	0.00	72.02	0
114	60a	0.53	28.84	58.58	0.27	0.00	15.82	4.11	11.71	0.00	0.00	0.00	15.82	0
115	60b	1.55	48.09	58.58	2.56	0.00	149.96	14.65	59.75	75.56	0.00	0.00	149.96	0
116	61	1.12	38.89	58.58	0.83	0.00	48.62	10.54	33.39	4.69	0.00	0.00	48.62	0
117	62a	0.20	28.84	58.58	0.10	0.00	5.86	1.76	4.10	0.00	0.00	0.00	5.86	0
118	62b	0.69	48.09	58.58	1.04	0.00	60.92	6.44	26.36	28.12	0.00	0.00	60.92	0
119	63	0.59	38.89	58.58	0.46	0.00	26.95	5.27	17.58	4.10	0.00	0.00	26.95	0
121	65	10.55	48.87	219.50	3.42	0.00	750.69	87.80	425.83	160.23	76.83	0.00	750.69	0
123	66	2.23	48.87	219.50	0.78	0.00	171.21	19.76	92.19	28.53	30.73	0.00	171.21	0
124	67	0.00	0.00	219.50	1.00	0.00	219.50	0.00	0.00	219.50	0.00	0.00	219.50	0
125	68a	0.30	28.84	3.00	2.90	0.00	8.70	2.34	6.36	0.00	0.00	0.00	8.70	0
126	68b	0.42	65.01	3.00	12.30	0.00	36.90	4.05	23.10	9.75	0.00	0.00	36.90	0
127	69a	0.10	28.84	1.00	2.90	0.00	2.90	0.78	2.12	0.00	0.00	0.00	2.90	0
128	69b	0.14	65.01	1.00	12.30	0.00	12.30	1.35	7.70	3.25	0.00	0.00	12.30	0
129	70a	0.10	28.84	1.00	2.90	0.00	2.90	0.78	2.12	0.00	0.00	0.00	2.90	0
130	70b	0.14	65.01	1.00	32.55	0.00	32.55	1.35	7.70	23.50	0.00	0.00	32.55	0
131	71a	0.19	28.84	2.00	2.71	0.00	5.42	1.46	3.96	0.00	0.00	0.00	5.42	0
132	71b	0.28	65.01	2.00	16.20	0.00	32.40	15.40	2.70	14.30	0.00	0.00	32.40	0
142	72a	1.84	28.84	221.06	0.25	0.00	55.27	39.79	15.48	0.00	0.00	0.00	55.27	0
143	72b	6.89	49.06	221.06	1.89	0.00	417.80	278.54	59.69	79.57	0.00	0.00	417.80	0
144	73a	3.64	24.84	436.56	0.25	0.00	109.14	78.58	30.56	0.00	0.00	0.00	109.14	0
145	73b	8.80	49.06	436.56	1.42	0.00	619.92	353.61	78.58	179.00	8.73	0.00	619.92	0
146	74	4.43	38.89	436.56	0.48	0.00	209.55	130.97	39.29	39.29	0.00	0.00	209.55	0
147	75	2.82	38.89	221.06	0.59	0.00	130.43	84.01	26.53	19.89	0.00	0.00	130.43	0
148	76a	2.31	28.84	327.42	0.21	0.00	68.76	49.12	19.64	0.00	0.00	0.00	68.76	0
149	76b	1.69	51.80	327.42	0.58	0.00	189.90	72.03	13.10	104.77	0.00	0.00	189.90	0
150	77a	0.38	28.84	1.00	10.89	0.00	10.89	7.96	2.93	0.00	0.00	0.00	10.89	0
151	77b	2.07	65.01	1.00	349.57	16.57	349.57	114.45	20.15	198.40	0.00	16.57	349.57	0
152	78	10.03	38.55	18.00	42.17	0.00	759.06	292.68	94.14	372.24	0.00	0.00	759.06	0
155	79	1.25	38.55	59.50	2.28	0.00	135.66	36.30	11.90	87.46	0.00	0.00	135.66	0
157	80	3.96	38.55	436.56	0.36	0.00	157.16	117.87	39.29	0.00	0.00	0.00	157.16	0
158	81a	1.61	28.84	160.00	0.29	0.00	46.40	33.60	12.80	0.00	0.00	0.00	46.40	0
159	81b	2.20	48.09	160.00	1.52	0.00	243.20	86.40	20.80	136.00	0.00	0.00	243.20	0
161	82	3.12	38.89	8.00	18.03	0.00	144.24	92.88	28.64	22.72	0.00	0.00	144.24	0
162	83	0.46	38.89	1.00	21.20	0.00	21.20	13.66	4.21	3.33	0.00	0.00	21.20	0
163	84a	1.61	28.84	8.00	5.81	0.00	46.48	34.00	12.48	0.00	0.00	0.00	46.48	0
164	84b	5.86	43.83	8.00	84.97	15.04	679.76	209.68	47.04	408.00	0.00	15.04	679.76	0
165	85a	0.20	28.84	1.00	5.81	0.00	5.81	4.25	1.56	0.00	0.00	0.00	5.81	0
166	85b	0.99	43.83	1.00	163.61	0.00	163.61	35.46	7.95	120.20	0.00	0.00	163.61	0
167	86a	0.49	28.84	53.58	0.27	0.00	14.47	10.71	3.76	0.00	0.00	0.00	14.47	0
168	86b	1.42	48.09	53.58	2.56	0.00	137.16	54.65	13.40	69.11	0.00	0.00	137.16	0
169	87	1.03	38.89	53.58	0.83	0.00	44.47	30.54	9.64	4.29	0.00	0.00	44.47	0
170	88a	0.30	28.84	1.00	8.66	0.00	8.66	6.33	2.33	0.00	0.00	0.00	8.66	0
171	88b	1.18	65.01	1.00	372.07	0.00	372.07	65.40	11.51	295.16	0.00	0.00	372.07	0

Adj#	Est#	Hrs	Rate	Qty	Unit Cost	Mkt Cond	Total	Burden	Labor	Matl	Eqpt	Mkt Cond	Total	Dif
172	89a	0.50	28.84	5.00	2.90	0.00	14.50	10.60	3.90	0.00	0.00	0.00	14.50	0
173	89b	0.70	65.01	5.00	12.30	0.00	61.50	38.50	6.75	16.25	0.00	0.00	61.50	0
174	90a	0.10	28.84	1.00	2.90	0.00	2.90	2.12	0.78	0.00	0.00	0.00	2.90	0
175	90b	0.14	65.01	1.00	12.30	0.00	12.30	7.70	1.35	3.25	0.00	0.00	12.30	0
176	91a	0.51	28.84	221.06	0.07	0.00	15.47	11.05	4.42	0.00	0.00	0.00	15.47	0
177	91b	0.34	53.00	221.06	0.81	24.32	179.06	15.47	2.21	137.06	0.00	24.32	179.06	0
178	92	1.20	28.84	221.06	0.15	0.00	33.16	24.31	8.85	0.00	0.00	0.00	33.16	0
179	93	2.42	53.00	239.00	3.12	0.00	745.68	107.55	21.51	602.28	14.34	0.00	745.68	0
187	94a	2.23	28.84	267.28	0.25	0.00	66.82	48.11	18.71	0.00	0.00	0.00	66.82	0
188	94b	8.33	49.06	267.28	1.89	0.00	505.16	336.77	72.17	96.22	0.00	0.00	505.16	0
189	95	3.01	38.89	267.28	0.78	58.81	208.48	90.87	26.73	32.07	0.00	58.81	208.48	0
190	96a	3.11	28.84	518.11	0.18	0.00	93.26	67.35	25.91	0.00	0.00	0.00	93.26	0
191	96b	12.79	48.09	518.11	1.81	0.00	937.78	492.21	124.35	321.22	0.00	0.00	937.78	0
192	97	4.51	38.89	310.87	0.68	0.00	211.39	133.67	40.41	37.31	0.00	0.00	211.39	0
193	98a	0.23	28.84	69.83	0.10	0.00	6.98	4.89	2.09	0.00	0.00	0.00	6.98	0
194	98b	0.82	48.09	69.83	0.98	0.00	68.43	31.42	7.68	29.33	0.00	0.00	68.43	0
195	99	0.89	38.89	69.83	0.56	0.00	39.10	26.54	8.38	4.18	0.00	0.00	39.10	0
196	100	5.02	38.55	9.00	42.17	0.00	379.53	146.34	47.07	186.12	0.00	0.00	379.53	0
197	101	2.04	38.55	225.00	0.36	0.00	81.00	60.75	20.25	0.00	0.00	0.00	81.00	0
198	102	5.26	38.89	518.11	0.48	0.00	248.69	155.43	46.63	46.63	0.00	0.00	248.69	0
199	103	1.88	38.89	147.28	0.59	0.00	86.90	55.96	17.67	13.27	0.00	0.00	86.90	0
200	104a	0.38	28.84	1.00	10.89	0.00	10.89	7.96	2.93	0.00	0.00	0.00	10.89	0
201	104b	2.07	65.01	1.00	219.60	0.38	219.60	114.45	20.15	84.62	0.00	0.38	219.60	0
202	105a	0.22	28.84	1.00	6.43	0.00	6.43	4.70	1.73	0.00	0.00	0.00	6.43	0
203	105b	0.91	65.01	1.00	88.63	0.00	88.63	50.24	8.84	29.55	0.00	0.00	88.63	0
204	106a	0.28	28.84	1.00	8.04	0.00	8.04	5.88	2.16	0.00	0.00	0.00	8.04	0
205	106b	0.52	65.01	1.00	57.56	0.00	57.56	28.64	5.04	23.88	0.00	0.00	57.56	0
206	107a	1.82	28.84	259.06	0.21	0.00	54.40	38.86	15.54	0.00	0.00	0.00	54.40	0
207	107b	1.33	51.80	259.06	0.58	0.00	150.25	57.00	10.36	82.89	0.00	0.00	150.25	0
208	108a	0.13	28.84	1.00	3.64	0.00	3.64	2.66	0.98	0.00	0.00	0.00	3.64	0
209	108b	0.69	48.09	1.00	89.76	1.22	89.76	26.51	6.53	55.50	0.00	1.22	89.76	0
211	109a	0.14	28.84	9.00	0.44	0.00	3.96	2.88	1.08	0.00	0.00	0.00	3.96	0
212	109b	0.50	48.09	9.00	5.21	0.00	46.89	19.26	4.77	22.86	0.00	0.00	46.89	0
213	110a	0.35	28.84	35.00	0.29	0.00	10.15	7.35	2.80	0.00	0.00	0.00	10.15	0
214	110b	0.48	48.09	35.00	1.52	0.00	53.20	18.90	4.55	29.75	0.00	0.00	53.20	0
215	111	1.10	23.00	3.00	8.45	0.00	25.35	19.38	5.91	0.06	0.00	0.00	25.35	0
216	112	1.64	38.89	3.00	25.40	0.00	76.20	48.63	15.00	12.57	0.00	0.00	76.20	0
217	113	1.95	38.89	5.00	18.03	0.00	90.15	58.05	17.90	14.20	0.00	0.00	90.15	0
218	114a	0.25	28.84	2.00	3.60	0.00	7.20	5.26	1.94	0.00	0.00	0.00	7.20	0
219	114b	1.66	50.97	2.00	242.37	0.00	484.74	68.58	16.16	400.00	0.00	0.00	484.74	0
221	115a	0.20	28.84	1.00	5.81	0.00	5.81	4.25	1.56	0.00	0.00	0.00	5.81	0
222	115b	0.73	43.83	1.00	84.97	1.88	84.97	26.21	5.88	51.00	0.00	1.88	84.97	0
23	116a	0.20	28.84	2.00	2.90	0.00	5.80	4.24	1.56	0.00	0.00	0.00	5.80	0
224	116b	1.46	43.83	2.00	77.49	0.00	154.98	52.42	11.76	90.80	0.00	0.00	154.98	0
225	117a	2.18	28.84	14.51	4.33	0.00	62.83	46.00	16.83	0.00	0.00	0.00	62.83	0
226	117b	7.74	48.09	14.51	99.62	0.00	1445.49	298.76	73.57	1073.16	0.00	0.00	1445.49	0
227	118a	0.22	28.84	5.11	1.24	0.00	6.34	4.65	1.69	0.00	0.00	0.00	6.34	0

Adj#	Est#	Hrs	Rate	Qty	Unit Cost	Mkt Cond	Total	Burden	Labor	Matl	Eqpt	Mkt Cond	Total	Dif
228	118b	0.35	48.09	5.11	43.26	0.00	221.06	13.39	3.27	204.40	0.00	0.00	221.06	0
229	119a	1.78	28.84	11.84	4.33	0.00	51.27	37.53	13.74	0.00	0.00	0.00	51.27	0
230	119b	6.32	48.09	11.84	162.23	0.00	1920.80	243.79	60.03	1616.98	0.00	0.00	1920.80	0
231	120a	0.47	28.84	12.00	1.12	0.00	13.44	9.84	3.60	0.00	0.00	0.00	13.44	0
232	120b	1.53	48.09	12.00	13.80	0.00	165.60	58.92	14.52	92.16	0.00	0.00	165.60	0
233	121a	1.22	28.84	14.17	2.49	0.00	35.28	25.79	9.49	0.00	0.00	0.00	35.28	0
234	121b	2.61	48.09	14.17	34.86	0.00	493.97	100.61	24.80	368.56	0.00	0.00	493.97	0
235	122	1.23	48.09	1.00	59.13	0.00	59.13	47.45	11.68	0.00	0.00	0.00	59.13	0
236	123a	0.25	28.84	14.17	0.52	0.00	7.37	5.39	1.98	0.00	0.00	0.00	7.37	0
237	123b	0.59	48.09	14.17	6.95	0.00	98.48	22.68	5.53	70.27	0.00	0.00	98.48	0
238	124	1.42	48.09	21.00	6.09	0.00	127.89	55.02	13.44	59.43	0.00	0.00	127.89	0
239	125a	40.00	28.84	1.00	11.54	0.00	11.54	8.44	3.10	0.00	0.00	0.00	11.54	0
240	125b	1.04	72.51	1.00	295.07	11.19	295.07	64.92	10.42	208.54	0.00	11.19	295.07	0
241	126a	0.37	28.84	1.00	10.82	0.00	10.82	7.91	2.91	0.00	0.00	0.00	10.82	0
242	126b	0.70	72.51	1.00	136.44	0.00	136.44	43.46	6.98	85.99	0.01	0.00	136.44	0
243	127a	0.50	28.84	1.00	14.43	0.00	14.43	10.55	3.88	0.00	0.00	0.00	14.43	0
244	127b	1.00	72.51	1.00	160.02	0.00	160.02	62.45	10.03	87.54	0.00	0.00	160.02	0
245	128a	0.54	28.84	1.00	15.45	0.00	15.45	11.30	4.15	0.00	0.00	0.00	15.45	0
246	128b	1.16	72.51	1.00	382.07	0.00	382.07	72.44	11.63	298.00	0.00	0.00	382.07	0
247	129a	40.00	28.84	1.00	11.62	0.00	11.62	8.50	3.12	0.00	0.00	0.00	11.62	0
248	129b	0.80	65.01	1.00	932.58	15.16	932.58	43.95	7.74	865.73	0.00	15.16	932.58	0
249	130a	0.13	28.84	1.00	3.64	0.00	3.64	2.66	0.98	0.00	0.00	0.00	3.64	0
250	130b	0.16	65.02	1.00	24.07	0.01	24.07	9.04	1.45	13.57	0.00	0.01	24.07	0
251	131b	0.06	28.84	2.00	0.81	0.00	1.62	1.18	0.44	0.00	0.00	0.00	1.62	0
252	131b	0.27	65.02	2.00	19.65	0.00	39.30	14.94	2.40	21.96	0.00	0.00	39.30	0
253	132a	0.58	28.84	63.75	0.27	0.00	17.21	12.76	4.45	0.00	0.00	0.00	17.21	0
254	132b	1.68	48.09	63.75	2.56	0.00	163.20	65.02	15.94	82.24	0.00	0.00	163.20	0
255	133	1.22	38.89	63.75	0.83	0.00	52.91	36.34	11.48	5.09	0.00	0.00	52.91	0
256	134a	0.21	28.84	63.75	0.10	0.00	6.38	4.47	1.91	0.00	0.00	0.00	6.38	0
257	134b	0.75	48.09	63.75	1.04	0.00	66.30	28.69	7.01	30.60	0.00	0.00	66.30	0
258	135	0.65	38.89	63.75	0.46	0.00	29.33	19.13	5.74	4.46	0.00	0.00	29.33	0
259	136a	0.50	28.84	5.00	2.90	0.00	14.50	10.60	3.90	0.00	0.00	0.00	14.50	0
260	136b	0.70	65.01	5.00	12.30	0.00	61.50	38.50	6.75	16.25	0.00	0.00	61.50	0
261	137a	0.60	28.84	6.00	2.90	0.00	17.40	12.72	4.68	0.00	0.00	0.00	17.40	0
262	137b	0.83	65.01	6.00	12.30	0.00	73.80	46.20	8.10	19.50	0.00	0.00	73.80	0
263	138a	0.09	28.84	1.00	2.60	0.00	2.60	1.90	0.70	0.00	0.00	0.00	2.60	0
264	138b	0.15	65.01	1.00	26.58	3.09	26.58	8.54	1.50	13.45	0.00	3.09	26.58	0
265	139a	0.10	28.84	1.00	2.90	0.00	2.90	2.12	0.78	0.00	0.00	0.00	2.90	0
266	139b	0.23	65.01	1.00	22.41	0.00	22.41	12.82	2.26	7.33	0.00	0.00	22.41	0
267	140a	0.19	28.84	2.00	2.71	0.00	5.42	3.96	1.46	0.00	0.00	0.00	5.42	0
268	140b	0.28	65.01	2.00	16.20	0.00	32.40	15.40	2.70	14.30	0.00	0.00	32.40	0
269	141a	2.25	53.00	120.00	0.99	0.00	118.80	99.60	19.20	0.00	0.00	0.00	118.80	0
270	141b	1.79	53.00	120.00	1.31	0.00	157.20	79.20	15.60	62.40	0.00	0.00	157.20	0
271	142	3.42	53.00	144.00	3.31	0.00	476.64	152.64	28.80	295.20	0.00	0.00	476.64	0
272	143a	0.38	28.84	165.00	0.07	0.00	11.55	8.25	3.30	0.00	0.00	0.00	11.55	0
273	143b	0.25	53.00	165.00	0.81	18.15	133.65	11.55	1.65	102.30	0.00	18.15	133.65	0
274	144a	0.90	28.84	165.00	0.15	0.00	24.75	18.15	6.60	0.00	0.00	0.00	24.75	0

Adj#	Est#	Hrs	Rate	Qty	Unit Cost	Mkt Cond	Total	Burden	Labor	Matl	Eqpt	Mkt Cond	Total	Dif
275	144b	1.67	53.00	165.00	3.12	0.00	514.80	74.25	14.85	415.80	9.90	0.00	514.80	0
276	145	0.53	53.00	165.00	0.17	0.00	28.05	23.10	4.95	0.00	0.00	0.00	28.05	0
277	146a	0.21	28.84	14.00	0.44	0.00	6.16	4.48	1.68	0.00	0.00	0.00	6.16	0
278	146b	0.27	53.00	14.00	3.12	0.00	43.68	11.90	2.24	29.54	0.00	0.00	43.68	0
291	147a	3.16	28.84	379.68	0.25	26.58	94.92	68.34	26.58	0.00	0.00	0.00	94.92	0
	147b	11.83	49.06	379.68	1.89	0.00	717.60	478.40	102.51	136.69	0.00	0.00	717.60	0
296	148	4.28	38.89	379.68	0.78	83.53	296.15	129.09	37.97	45.56	0.00	83.53	296.15	0
297	149a	0.17	28.84	1.00	4.81	0.00	4.81	3.52	1.29	0.00	0.00	0.00	4.81	0
298	149b	0.38	65.01	1.00	51.58	2.53	51.58	21.02	3.70	24.33	0.00	2.53	51.58	0
299	150	0.34	65.01	1.00	35.81	0.00	35.81	18.96	3.34	13.51	0.00	0.00	35.81	0
300	151a	0.43	28.84	1.00	12.35	0.00	12.35	9.03	3.32	0.00	0.00	0.00	12.35	0
301	151b	1.19	48.09	1.00	435.15	0.00	435.15	45.74	11.26	378.15	0.00	0.00	435.15	0
303	152	1.78	48.09	1.00	126.95	0.00	126.95	68.60	16.89	41.46	0.00	0.00	126.95	0
304	153	0.46	43.83	1.00	71.39	5.54	71.39	16.61	3.72	45.52	0.00	5.54	71.39	0
305	154a	0.35	28.84	1.00	10.18	0.00	10.18	7.44	2.74	0.00	0.00	0.00	10.18	0
306	154b	1.33	48.09	1.00	234.27	0.00	234.27	51.47	12.67	170.13	0.00	0.00	234.27	0
307	155a	0.37	28.84	1.00	10.82	0.00	10.82	7.91	2.91	0.00	0.00	0.00	10.82	0
308	155b	0.79	48.09	1.00	155.53	9.91	155.53	30.49	7.51	107.62	0.00	9.91	155.53	0
309	156a	0.25	28.84	1.00	7.22	0.00	7.22	5.28	1.94	0.00	0.00	0.00	7.22	0
310	156b	0.35	43.83	1.00	36.01	0.00	36.01	12.45	2.79	20.77	0.00	0.00	36.01	0
311	157	1.35	38.89	4.00	17.85	0.04	71.40	40.24	12.40	18.72	0.00	0.04	71.40	0
312	158	1.17	38.89	3.00	18.03	0.00	54.09	34.83	10.74	8.52	0.00	0.00	54.09	0
313	159a	0.52	28.84	5.17	2.89	0.00	14.94	10.91	4.03	0.00	0.00	0.00	14.94	0
314	159b	1.72	48.09	5.17	20.32	0.00	105.05	66.49	16.39	22.17	0.00	0.00	105.05	0
315	160	0.67	38.89	1.00	30.45	0.00	30.45	20.03	6.18	4.24	0.00	0.00	30.45	0
316	161	3.26	38.89	321.45	0.48	0.00	154.30	96.44	28.93	28.93	0.00	0.00	154.30	0
	162	0.74	38.89	58.24	0.59	0.00	34.36	22.13	6.99	5.24	0.00	0.00	34.36	0
	163a	0.15	28.84	21.00	0.21	0.00	4.41	3.15	1.26	0.00	0.00	0.00	4.41	0
	163b	0.11	51.80	21.00	0.58	0.00	12.18	4.62	0.84	6.72	0.00	0.00	12.18	0
	164a	0.04	28.84	39.67	0.27	0.00	10.71	7.93	2.78	0.00	0.00	0.00	10.71	0
317	164b	1.05	48.09	39.67	2.56	0.00	101.56	40.46	9.92	51.18	0.00	0.00	101.56	0
318	165	0.76	38.89	39.67	0.83	0.00	32.93	22.61	7.14	3.18	0.00	0.00	32.93	0
319	166a	0.13	28.84	39.67	0.10	0.00	3.97	2.77	1.20	0.00	0.00	0.00	3.97	0
320	166b	0.47	48.09	39.67	1.04	0.00	41.26	17.85	4.36	19.05	0.00	0.00	41.26	0
321	167	0.40	38.89	39.67	0.46	0.00	18.25	11.90	3.57	2.78	0.00	0.00	18.25	0
322	168a	0.30	28.84	3.00	2.90	0.00	8.70	6.36	2.34	0.00	0.00	0.00	8.70	0
323	168b	0.42	65.01	3.00	12.30	0.00	36.90	23.10	4.05	9.75	0.00	0.00	36.90	0
324	169	1.02	25.25	58.24	0.53	0.00	30.87	20.38	5.82	4.67	0.00	0.00	30.87	0
327	170a	1.14	28.84	137.35	0.25	0.00	34.34	24.73	9.61	0.00	0.00	0.00	34.34	0
328	170b	4.28	49.06	137.35	1.89	0.00	259.59	173.06	37.08	49.45	0.00	0.00	259.59	0
329	171	1.55	38.89	137.35	0.78	30.21	107.13	46.70	13.74	16.48	0.00	30.21	107.13	0
330	172a	0.17	28.84	1.00	4.81	0.00	4.81	3.52	1.29	0.00	0.00	0.00	4.81	0
331	172b	0.25	65.01	1.00	21.43	0.00	21.43	13.83	2.43	5.17	0.00	0.00	21.43	0
332	173a	0.12	28.84	15.50	0.22	0.00	3.41	2.49	0.92	0.00	0.00	0.00	3.41	0
333	173b	1.29	48.09	15.50	7.32	0.00	113.46	49.76	12.25	51.45	0.00	0.00	113.46	0
334	174	0.70	38.89	15.50	2.10	0.00	32.55	20.93	6.51	5.11	0.00	0.00	32.55	0
335	175a	0.30	28.84	1.00	8.66	0.00	8.66	6.33	2.33	0.00	0.00	0.00	8.66	0

Adj#	Est#	Hrs	Rate	Qty	Unit Cost	Mkt Cond	Total	Burden	Labor	Matl	Eqpt	Mkt Cond	Total	Dif
336	175b	1.33	48.09	1.00	181.14	0.00	181.14	51.47	12.67	117.00	0.00	0.00	181.14	0
337	176	3.69	38.89	4.00	45.75	0.00	183.00	109.72	33.84	39.44	0.00	0.00	183.00	0
338	177a	0.10	28.84	1.00	2.90	0.00	2.90	2.12	0.78	0.00	0.00	0.00	2.90	0
339	177b	0.34	65.02	1.00	46.78	0.00	46.78	18.89	3.03	24.86	0.00	0.00	46.78	0
340	178	1.26	38.89	124.00	0.48	0.00	59.52	37.20	11.16	11.16	0.00	0.00	59.52	0
341	179	0.17	38.89	13.35	0.59	0.00	7.88	5.07	1.60	1.21	0.00	0.00	7.88	0
342	180a	0.14	28.84	15.50	0.27	0.00	4.19	3.10	1.09	0.00	0.00	0.00	4.19	0
343	180b	0.41	48.09	15.50	2.56	0.00	39.68	15.82	3.88	19.98	0.00	0.00	39.68	0
344	181	0.30	38.89	15.50	0.83	0.00	12.87	8.84	2.79	1.24	0.00	0.00	12.87	0
345	182a	0.05	28.84	15.50	0.10	0.00	1.55	1.09	0.46	0.00	0.00	0.00	1.55	0
346	182b	0.18	48.09	15.50	1.04	0.00	16.12	6.98	1.71	7.43	0.00	0.00	16.12	0
347	183	0.16	38.89	15.50	0.46	0.00	7.13	4.65	1.40	1.08	0.00	0.00	7.13	0
348	184a	0.25	53.00	13.35	0.99	0.00	13.22	11.08	2.14	0.00	0.00	0.00	13.22	0
349	184b	0.20	53.00	13.35	1.31	0.00	17.49	8.81	1.74	6.94	0.00	0.00	17.49	0
350	185	0.09	53.00	13.35	0.47	0.12	6.27	4.01	0.80	1.34	0.00	0.12	6.27	0
351	186	0.21	53.00	13.35	1.79	0.00	23.90	9.35	1.87	12.68	0.00	0.00	23.90	0
352	187a	3.41	28.84	409.60	0.25	0.00	102.40	73.73	28.67	0.00	0.00	0.00	102.40	0
353	187b	12.77	49.06	409.60	1.89	28.84	774.14	516.09	110.59	147.46	0.00	0.00	774.14	0
	188	4.62	38.89	409.60	0.78	90.11	319.49	139.27	40.96	49.15	0.00	90.11	319.49	0
354	189a	0.17	28.84	1.00	4.81	0.00	4.81	3.52	1.29	0.00	0.00	0.00	4.81	0
355	189b	0.38	65.01	1.00	51.58	0.00	51.58	21.02	3.70	24.33	0.00	2.53	51.58	0
356	190a	0.22	28.84	1.00	6.40	0.00	6.40	4.68	1.72	0.00	0.00	0.00	6.40	0
357	190b	0.34	65.01	1.00	35.81	0.00	35.81	18.96	3.34	13.51	0.00	0.00	35.81	0
358	191a	0.25	28.84	1.00	7.23	0.00	7.23	5.29	1.94	0.00	0.00	0.00	7.23	0
359	191	4.55	65.02	1.00	517.37	0.00	517.37	254.69	40.86	221.82	0.00	0.00	517.37	0
360	192a	0.10	28.84	1.00	2.90	0.00	2.90	2.12	0.78	0.00	0.00	0.00	2.90	0
361	192b	1.04	65.01	1.00	98.41	0.00	98.41	57.27	10.08	31.06	0.00	0.00	98.41	0
362	193a	0.11	28.84	1.00	3.21	0.00	3.21	2.35	0.86	0.00	0.00	0.00	3.21	0
363	193b	0.50	65.02	1.00	142.84	0.00	142.84	28.04	4.50	110.30	0.00	0.00	142.84	0
364	194	3.63	38.89	358.00	0.48	0.00	171.84	107.40	32.22	32.22	0.00	0.00	171.84	0
365	195	0.66	38.89	51.60	0.59	0.00	30.44	19.61	6.19	4.64	0.00	0.00	30.44	0
366	196a	0.13	28.84	1.00	3.64	0.00	3.64	2.66	0.98	0.00	0.00	0.00	3.64	0
367	196b	0.16	65.02	1.00	24.07	0.01	24.07	9.04	1.45	13.57	0.00	0.01	24.07	0
368	197a	0.72	28.84	4.00	5.20	0.00	20.80	15.20	5.60	0.00	0.00	0.00	20.80	0
369	197b	2.70	48.09	4.00	236.91	0.00	947.64	104.24	25.68	817.72	0.00	0.00	947.64	0
371	198	2.31	38.89	4.00	29.79	0.00	119.16	68.76	21.20	29.20	0.00	0.00	119.16	0
372	199a	0.09	28.84	4.00	0.67	0.00	2.68	1.96	0.72	0.00	0.00	0.00	2.68	0
373	199b	0.27	48.09	4.00	6.09	0.00	24.36	10.48	2.56	11.32	0.00	0.00	24.36	0
	517	24.84	23.00	2949.25	0.21	0.00	619.34	442.39	147.46	29.49	0.00	0.00	619.34	0
	518	8.00	23.00	8.00	23.00	0.00	184.00	141.04	42.96	0.00	0.00	0.00	184.00	0

This worksheet compares the values in the two estimates looking for any discrepancies. The ideal is to end up with Dif = 0 on each line.

ABOUT THE AUTHOR

Joe Kidd and his wife experienced a home fire several years ago. Having gone through the process of recovery and rebuilding, he decided to put the principles of data analytics, process and project management to help others to have the same experiences and to prepare everyone else. With 40 plus years of experience in data analytics, insurance sales, marketing, process/project management and publishing, he is uniquely positioned to offer a new perspective on the residential insurance claims and reconciliation processes.